FIRST MANASSAS 1861

FIRST MANASSAS 1861

THE BATTLE OF BULL RUN

ALAN HANKINSON

◀ Climax of the battle:
what the Northern
soldiers had to face as they
attacked up Henry Hill,
though this artist has
exaggerated considerably
the angle of slope.

First published in Great Britain in
1990 by Osprey Publishing,
Elms Court, Chapel Way, Botley,
Oxford OX2 9LP, United
Kingdom.
Email: info@ospreypublishing.com

© Copyright 1990
Osprey Publishing Ltd.
Reprinted 1993, 1996(twice),
1998, 1999, 2000

Also published as Campaign 10
First Bull Run 1861

Produced by DAG Publications Ltd
for Osprey Publishing Ltd.
Colour bird's eye view illustrations
by Cilla Eurich.
Tourist information by Adam Ward

Back cover Cartography by
The Map Studio

Wargaming First Bull Run 1861 by
Arthur Harman.
Wargames consultant Duncan
Macfarlane.
Typeset by Ronset Typesetters Ltd,
Darwen, Lancashire
Mono camerawork by M&E
Reproductions, North Fambridge,
Essex.
Printed in China

ISBN 1 84176 1133

FOR A CATALOGUE OF ALL
BOOKS PUBLISHED BY OSPREY
MILITARY, AUTOMOTIVE AND
AVIATION PLEASE WRITE TO:

The Marketing Manager,
Osprey Direct UK, PO Box 140,
Wellingborough, Northants,
NN8 4ZA, United Kingdom
Email: info@OspreyDirect.co.uk

The Marketing Manager, Osprey
Direct USA, PO Box 130, Sterling
Heights, MI 48311-0130, USA.
Email: info@OspreyDirectUSA.com

Visit Osprey at:
www.ospreypublishing.com

FRONT COVER
***A dramatic 'artist's
impression' of the clash
between Stuart's cavalry
and the New York Zouaves
on Henry Hill. (Anne S. K.
Brown Mil. Coll., BUL)***

CONTENTS

Key to Map Symbols

Army	⊠ (xxxx)
Corps	⊠ (xxx)
Division	⊠ (xx)
Brigade	⊠ (x)
Regiment	⊠ (iii)
Battalion	⊠ (ii)
Cavalry	◰

INTRODUCTION

Bull Run is a pleasant, gently flowing river in northern Virginia, which runs through rolling green farmland on its way to join the Potomac. By American standards it is not much of a river, but it is wide and deep enough to present problems to an army on the move. The United States capital, Washington, is some 25 miles away to the north-east. The city of Richmond, Virginia, which became the capital of the break-away Confederate states in 1861, lies 80 miles or so to the south. The fact that it lay between these opposing capitals, abetted by the fact that it was close to the railway junction of Manassas, meant that a few acres of this peaceful countryside formed the stage for two fierce battles within the first fourteen months of the American Civil War.

The First Battle of Bull Run is significant for several reasons. It was the first major encounter of the war, and it is possible that had victory gone to the North, as it very nearly did, then the war – which was to go on for nearly four more years and to claim the lives of more than 600,000 men – might have ended then. It was the first battle ever fought in which the movement of men by railway played an influential part. And it taught both sides that they were in for a long struggle, which would not be won merely by dash and gallantry.

From the military point of view, the lessons it taught were negative. Neither army was ready for battle; the men were untrained, the commanders inexperienced. There was no inspired generalship. The issue was decided more by luck than by anybody's good management. It was a demonstration, more than anything else, of all-round military incompetence.

◄ *Scene of the battle's turning-point: the slopes leading up to Henry House and the summit plateau. The slight depression in the ground, where the trees stand, afforded the attacking Northern regiments a little cover, but once they were over the crest they came under withering fire from Jackson's line.*

THE WAY TO CIVIL WAR

Hollywood films have conditioned the world to see the United States of America in the first half of the nineteenth century as a land of violence – bitter feuds and banditry, shoot-outs and lynch mobs, and incessant Indian wars. English visitors at the time, such as Frances Trollope, Harriet Martineau and Charles Dickens, portrayed it as a crude and mannerless society, full of tobacco-chewers and spitoons, loud with drunks and their public brawling. In fact, though, to most of those who lived there then, and especially the hundreds of thousands who had recently escaped from the persecutions and deprivations of Europe, it was a land of boundless opportunity and optimism. The United States was a young country, still united, comparatively peaceful and, by world standards at the time, highly democratic. It was also prosperous and expanding. The population was growing rapidly. Vast new territories were constantly being added to the Union, with broad rivers and fertile plains and hills that were rich in minerals. A complex network of railways sprang up to make transport easier and faster. In the North, towns were growing into cities and many new industries were appearing. Every ship that arrived from across the Atlantic brought hundreds more immigrants from the 'old world', most of them young, many of them with specialist skills, all of them ambitious to make their fortunes in this 'brave new world'. The society they joined was tough and competitive. The rewards went to those who were strong and resourceful and ready to work hard. But the prizes were worth the winning and, compared with the countries they had left behind, there was remarkable freedom to pursue them.

But the very speed with which the country was growing and changing created strains. In a sense, three different countries were emerging. The West, where new territories were continuously opening up, was the place for pioneers; life there was primitive; families and communities had to be tough and self-reliant. The North-East was much more settled and it was here that towns were growing into cities and new industries were springing up. All was change and bustle in this region as descendants of the original colonists, mostly English, were joined by a heady ethnic mix of Italians and Irish, Scots and Germans, Slavs and Scandinavians and others. And the South was another world entirely, a near-tropical land of great plantations where white land-owners enjoyed a privileged and leisurely way of life. Unlike the other two regions, society here was static, rigidly based on conventions, fixed and hierarchical.

There were not only wide differences in character and climate; there were conflicts of interest too. The North, for example, wanted high tariff barriers against imports from abroad to protect nascent industries from European competition. But the South, heavily dependent on exports of cotton and tobacco to Europe, wanted free trade. Many Southerners feared, with good reason, that it was only a matter of time before the population disparity would be such that their interests would be over-ridden by the other parts of the Union. As early as the 1820s there had been talk, among the more extreme elements in the South, of secession, breaking away from the Union to go it alone.

The Slavery Issue

Even so, the majority of Americans cherished the notion of their country's 'manifest destiny', the idea that the push westwards would be maintained until they had built a vast and powerful nation 'from sea to shining sea'. The power of this vision, and the regard many held for the founding fathers and the unique democratic republic they had created, would almost certainly have held the country together had it not been for one further factor: the institution of chattel slavery.

By 1860 there were well over three million negro slaves in the southern states, most of them labouring on the plantations. The invention of the cotton gin, making the short-staple cotton that grew so abundantly there suitable for processing in the textile mills of Europe, paved the way for a lucrative export industry. In 1860 cotton represented 57 per cent of the value of all America's exports. The business was based on the labour of the slaves, descendants of West African tribespeople who had been shipped across the Atlantic in colonial times. The slaves were property – bought and sold at the markets, owned and entirely controlled by their white masters.

Slavery had died out in the northern states, for economic rather than for moral reasons. But, as the years passed, an increasing and increasingly vocal body of opinion grew up, demanding that slavery be abolished throughout the Union. By the middle of the nineteenth century, however, this was still a minority feeling. Most moderate opinion in the North, however much it disapproved of slavery in principle, was prepared to accept its existence in the South as a fact that had to be recognized. And most reasonable men in the South were happy enough to stay in the Union so long as there were no direct attempts to end the system by which they lived.

Unfortunately, there was a further complication. What should be the rule about the new states that were constantly joining the union? Should they be slave states or not? Should the question be determined simply by latitude, their geographical position? Or by some kind of plebiscite? Or imposed by Congress in Washington?

The issue arose over Missouri in the 1820s and there was long and heated argument. It surfaced again in the late 1840s when the defeat of Mexico brought extensive new territories into the Union. Feelings grew stronger and the language used more intemperate. Various solutions were devised and tried, found wanting and replaced by ever more complex compromises. By this time the fiercer opponents of slavery were organizing an 'underground railroad' to help disaffected slaves escape to the North. Southern landowners saw this as a direct assault on their livelihoods. The debate intensified and it grew ever harder to hold to a middle view. When *Uncle Tom's Cabin* was published in book form in 1852, its portrayal of plantation life was deeply resented in the South – but it sold 300,000 copies, mostly in the North, in the first year.

In the 1850s the accession of another new state, Kansas, brought a further intensification of the dispute. There was ballot-rigging and mass-intimidation. Gun-fights took place in the townships and armed gangs from neighbouring states, of both persuasions, raided across the border. In May 1856 a member of the national legislature, a senator from Massachusetts who had made a bitter anti-slavery speech, was attacked on the floor of the House, beaten to the ground with a heavy stick and badly injured by an irate congressman from South Carolina. Two days later a fanatical Ohio farmer, John Brown, led four of his sons and three other zealots on a night raid into Kansas and hacked to death with swords and daggers the first five men they found, assuming them to be slavers. More and more people in the South were beginning to say they would never enjoy peace until they broke away from the Union.

In October 1859, John Brown struck again, gaining himself immortality in song. With a handful of supporters he seized the Federal arsenal at Harpers Ferry in West Virginia. They planned to use the arms to stimulate a general insurrection of the slaves in the South. But their inept attempt was smartly dealt with by a detachment of US Marines led by a colonel called Robert E. Lee. Brown was tried, convicted of treason and hanged. From this moment on, the pace of events quickened ominously.

The next year, 1860, was presidential election year. The former political parties were in flux. The old Whig party had been replaced by a new force, the Republicans, representing Northern interests and opinion. Initially the Democrats, who spoke for the Southern whites, seemed in better shape, but when their delegates gathered at Charleston in April to choose their party's candidate, the meeting collapsed into a ferocious row between extremists and moderates, and in the end they split asunder, each group putting up a presidential candidate.

The Republicans, at their convention in Chicago, were also divided; but, aware that the disarray of their opponents gave their candidate an excellent chance, they finally reached an agreed choice. It was a momentous one. Their candidate was a big, strong, gangling, odd-mannered frontiersman, with little in the way of formal education but a formidable natural intelligence, a man of high integrity and astonishing powers of persuasion – Abraham Lincoln.

During his campaign for the presidency, Lincoln did everything he could to reassure the Southerners that if he won he would do nothing to threaten the institution of slavery where it already existed. Personally, he did not approve of slavery, but he prized the continued union of the United States above all else and knew that the one sure way of breaking the country up was to make the Southern system feel endangered.

The Confederacy

The South was not, however, reassured. Lincoln won the race for the White House, through the divisions among his rivals. The result was known in November 1860. Next month South Carolina, always the most extreme of the Southern states, voted to secede from the United States. Before the end of January 1861, six more states had left the Union: Mississippi, Alabama, Georgia, Florida, Louisiana and Texas. Their delegates met at Montgomery, Alabama, on 8 February and agreed to join together to form a new country to be called the Confederate States of America. They drafted a constitution and next day elected their own president, Jefferson Davis of Mississippi. There were Federal forts and arsenals within their territories and most of these were promptly taken over, without bloodshed.

Lincoln went to Washington and was sworn in as president on 4 March. In his Inaugural Address he tried to woo back the seven break-away states. 'We are not enemies, but friends,' he told them. 'We must not be enemies. Though passion may have strained, it must not break our bonds of affection.' He went on to say that his forces would never start the shooting. If civil war were to come, they, the Southerners, would have to launch it.

▲ *Abraham Lincoln, regarded by many as one of the greatest men who ever lived, had only just become President of the Union when it began to break up. He was not, at first, an outright opponent of the slave system – he thought each state should be allowed to choose for itself – but he put the preservation of the Union above all other considerations. He had virtually no military experience but became a formidable leader in war. He saw it through to final victory, and was beginning to work for the healing of the wounds of Civil War when he was assassinated by John Wilkes Booth in April 1865. (Anne S. K. Brown Mil. Coll., BUL)*

The response was unpromising. On 6 March, Jefferson Davis asked his confederate states to provide him with 100,000 volunteers for one year's military service. Five weeks later Southern guns opened fire on Fort Sumter, on an island near the mouth of Charleston harbour in South Carolina. This was one of the Federal army forts that had not been taken; it still flew the Union flag, and this was seen as an insult to the South. On 8 April, Lincoln sent a message to Jefferson Davis, saying that he planned to send a supply ship to Fort Sumter and promising that it would only deliver food to the garrison. Davis told his commander in

Union and Confederate: opposing states, July 1861

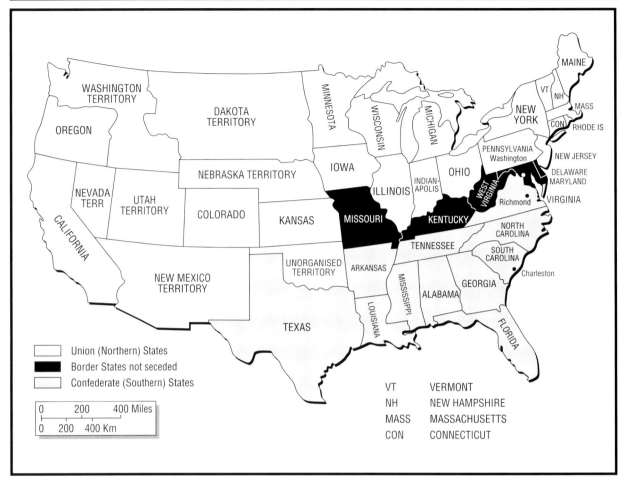

Union (Northern) States
Border States not seceded
Confederate (Southern) States

0   200   400 Miles
0   200   400 Km

VT   VERMONT
NH   NEW HAMPSHIRE
MASS   MASSACHUSETTS
CON   CONNECTICUT

the region, General P.G.T. Beauregard, to demand the immediate surrender of the garrison and, if this were not promptly forthcoming, to open fire. On 12 April, Beauregard's guns opened up; 34 hours later the garrison hauled down the 'Stars and Stripes' and surrendered. Not a man had been killed in the brief action, but everyone knew that this was the start of civil war.

To most people on both sides the outbreak of hostilities brought a welcome sense of relief. The long years of abuse, recrimination and threats were over. The matter would now be settled by combat. There was much public celebration, North and South, and a common conviction that the war would not last long and that they would be the victors.

Lincoln himself must have shared this optimistic view because he now asked the states loyal to

the Union to raise 75,000 volunteers to serve for a period of only three months – an underestimate that was to influence the outcome of the First Battle of Bull Run.

Two days after the President issued that call, the key state of Virginia opted to join the breakaway – then three more states that had been neutral so far, North Carolina, Tennessee and Arkansas, brought the total number of confederate states to eleven.

So the battle lines were drawn. The statistics favoured the North: they had a total population of more than eighteen million, twice the number in the South, of which more than a third were slaves who could hardly be expected to fight for their continued subjugation. The great bulk of manufacturing power lay in the Northern states; most of the useful minerals; two-thirds of the railways; and virtually all the naval power. If it were to be a long war, there could be little doubt who would prevail.

The Southerners began the war convinced that their moral (and *morale*) advantages outweighed the material advantages of the enemy. Northerners, they believed, had been softened by their more urban and industrialized lives. It was a widely-stated claim that any Southern man 'could lick five Yankees'. And although it was their guns that had opened the firing, Southerners saw themselves as the victims of aggression. All they wanted was to go their separate way in peace. The North was seeking to conquer them. Most of the fighting would be done on Southern soil – they were defending their homeland. When this happens (as the Americans were to find in Vietnam;

the Russians in Afghanistan, a century later) the key factor is not firepower but will power. Many Southerners also thought that Europe's dependence on their cotton would ultimately bring Britain, and possibly France as well, into the war on their side.

Soon after Virginia joined the Confederacy, Jefferson Davis moved his headquarters from Montgomery to the Virginia state capital, Richmond, within a hundred miles of Washington. In his *History of the English-speaking Peoples*, Winston Churchill commented: 'Thus the two capitals stood like queens at chess upon adjoining squares, and, sustained by their combinations of covering pieces, they endured four years of grim play within a single move of capture.'

▼ *South Carolina, always the most bellicose of the Southern states, declared itself separated from the United States in December 1860, soon after hearing the news that Lincoln had been elected President of the Union. Six more Southern states were quick to follow South Carolina. They proclaimed themselves a new country – the Confederate States of America – and by the time the First Battle of Bull Run was fought, there were eleven states in the CSA.*

▼ *The proud old state of Virginia agonized for many weeks over whether it should break away from the Union or not. When the decision to secede was finally taken, however, many of the Union army's best officers – who were Virginians and put their state before their country – resigned to serve in the Confederate Army. The call went out for volunteer soldiers to sign on for one year's service, and the response was enthusiastic.*

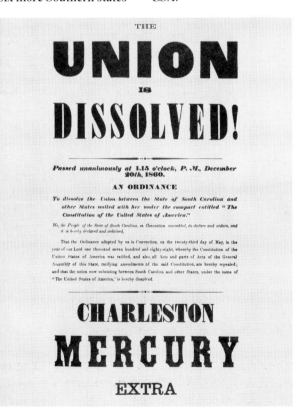

THE OPPOSING LEADERS

The two American presidents who now confronted each other had similar origins – they were both born close to the River Ohio in Kentucky, Jefferson Davis in June 1808, Lincoln some eight months later. Both grew up to be tall and lean, with the bony, angular, strong-jawed features that seem to have been fashionable at that period. They were men of intelligence and probity. Each of them went into politics and prospered and spoke, by the standards of the time, for the forces of reason and moderation. They were both family men.

But there the similarities end. Davis moved South to become a Mississippi planter while Lincoln went in the other direction and, after a variety of jobs, settled down as a small-town lawyer in Springfield, Illinois. Davis was a man of severe manner and rigid mind, with little in the way of humour or social warmth, a forbidding boss, always very sure that he was in the right. Lincoln, by contrast, was relaxed and folksy and often funny, modest in manner and – although a man of deep thought and conviction – flexible in his approach. He was the consummate politician, charming and persuasive in private meetings and committees, compelling and persuasive in his public utterances.

On the face of it, judging from their experience, Davis should have made the better war leader. At the age of 16 he had gone to study at West Point Military Academy, to emerge four years later as a second lieutenant in the US Army. He served for seven years and saw action against the 'Black Hawk' Indians. He then retired from the army to marry and become a cotton planter and a politician. He re-enlisted, however, for the Mexican War and, as colonel of the volunteer Mississippi Rifles, distinguished himself in action at the Battle of Monterey and then joined the staff of General Zachary Taylor. Returning to national politics after the war, he was President Pierce's Secretary of War in the mid-1850s. Davis had known war at many levels and in many of its aspects.

Lincoln could claim no such qualifications. He was a man of great strength and courage – a formidable opponent, by all accounts, in a fight – but his military experience was negligible. In 1833 he had volunteered for a minor Indian war, was elected captain of the local militia, marched his men about the countryside briefly but saw no action at all and was glad to get back to civilian life. But if Lincoln could point to no obvious qualifications for the task he now faced, he did have, in full measure, the qualities that Clausewitz said were of most importance to the director of a war – 'a remarkable, superior mind and strength of character'.

The Chief Military Advisers

In the event, Davis was not to prove as able a wartime commander as Lincoln, but he had one important initial advantage. His military right-hand-man from the beginning of the conflict was Robert E. Lee, a man of high distinction. Lee came from a proud Virginian family; his father had been a hero of the War of Independence. The boy studied at West Point, became an officer in the engineers, fought in the Mexican War and rose to the rank of colonel, then returned to West Point as its commanding officer. He was handsome and civilized as well as an able soldier, and won the love as well as the respect of those who served under him. He was 54 in 1861. The break-up of the United States deeply distressed him: 'I can contemplate no greater calamity for the country', he said, 'than a dissolution of the Union.' But when the dissolution came and Virginia voted to join the Confederacy, it was his love for his native state that prevailed. Had he stayed with the Union,

▲ Jefferson Davis, elected President of the CSA in February 1861, had been a professional soldier, a cotton planter, a successful politician, and in the 1850s Secretary of War to President Pierce in Washington. A man of great integrity, sincerity and resolution, he lacked Lincoln's geniality of manner and flexibility of mind. He was taken prisoner in May 1865, as the war was ending, and spent two years in gaol, for some time under threat of being tried for treason. After his release, he retired to his estates in Mississippi and took no further part in politics. He died in 1889. (From an oil painting by John Robertson)

▲ Robert E. Lee, who came from a very distinguished Virginian family, might well have become Lincoln's commander-in-chief in 1861 had he not opted for his state and the Confederacy. As it was, Jefferson Davis quickly made him his chief military adviser. He played no active part in First Bull Run, but later proved his worth as a commander in the field as well as in the realm of grand strategy. It was his determination and skill, more than any other factor, that kept the Southern cause alive and kicking for so long. He was respected by his enemies, respected and loved by his own men. He died in October 1870. (Anne S. K. Brown Mil. Coll., BUL)

it seems more than likely that he would have been offered command of Lincoln's main army in the field. As soon as he had thrown in his lot with the South, Davis made him a general and appointed him his chief military adviser. He was to serve, as adviser and field commander, throughout the war.

Lincoln's chief military adviser was another Virginian and one with an even more impressive record than Lee. Lieutenant General Winfield Scott had fought against the British in the War of 1812 and was general-in-chief of the US Army in 1847 when he brilliantly led the invasion of Mexico. When the Civil War began there was never any doubt that he would stay loyal to the Union, but he was 74 years old by that time and in poor health. A very tall man, he was now very fat as well, so much so that he could no longer get on to a horse and walked with difficulty. Sometimes his mind seemed as strong and sharp as it had ever been, but there were also times when his thoughts wandered and his orders grew vague and confused. He had less control over his temper than formerly; he could be proud and prickly; too often he let personal considerations affect his military judgement. The sad fact is that Winfield Scott was too old and tired for the immense responsibilities he was now given.

Such were the four top men – Lincoln and Scott for the North, Davis and Lee for the South. Each of them had some say in the build-up to the First Battle of Bull Run but none of them was involved in the battle itself. This was the work, in varying degrees, of four generals – Irvin McDowell and Robert Patterson on the Northern side, Joseph E. Johnston and P.G.T. Beauregard on the Southern.

The Field Commanders

The action at Fort Sumter was short and simple and quite unheroic, but after it Pierre Gustave Toutant Beauregard was acclaimed throughout the jubilant South as the 'Hero of Sumter'. It was typical of the man, never one to pass up a chance for further self-aggrandisement. It was one of the qualities he shared with his own hero, Napoleon Bonaparte; strategic and tactical instruction at West Point was largely geared to the precepts and example of the great French commander, and none took the lessons more to heart than Beauregard. He loved the Napoleonic ceremonial and style. He saw himself, some said, as a reincarnation of one of the more dashing of the marshals. He was bouncing with confidence and energy, a great favourite with the ladies, and something of a swaggerer.

Beauregard came of mixed lineage, French and Welsh. He was of medium height and swarthy

▲ *In 1861 the military record of General Winfield Scott was unparalleled in the United States. He had fought against the British in 1812, and his conduct of the invasion of Mexico in 1847 had made him a national hero. He was one of the few prominent Virginians who chose to stay in the Union army. Unfortunately, by the summer of* 1861 he was in his mid-seventies and in poor physical shape. He was not on the field at First Bull Run, but the confused and over-cautious orders he sent to General Patterson were partly responsible for the defeat of the North. After the battle he faded from the scene and died five years later. (Anne S. K. Brown Mil. Coll., BUL)

▲ *Pierre Gustave Toutant Beauregard was a general whose charismatic flamboyance, confidence and ambition were not matched by strategic skill. His schemes were often ill-advised; his orders unclear. He went to Manassas as 'the Hero of Sumter' and emerged from the Bull Run battle with his reputation even further enhanced. He* continued to be actively engaged in the Civil War but never fulfilled the promise of the opening months of the war. He lived until 1893 (Anne S. K. Brown Mil. Coll., BUL)

▶ *There is nothing like war for stimulating interest in the news. Frank Vitzetelli, an artist who had been sent out by the* Illustrated London News, *caught something of the excitement of a mixed New York group in the weeks before Bull Run when the newspapers were calling for an attack on the South. (*Illustrated London News, *15 June 1861)*

complexion, with a touch of the exotic in his appearance and manner. His family owned slaves and ran large sugar cane plantations in Louisiana. He did well in his studies at West Point, was commissioned into the engineers and served on Winfield Scott's staff in the Mexican War. He ended the war as a major, full of ambition. But the years that followed were uneventful.

He was 43 when the Civil War broke out. This was his big opportunity. He had made no secret of his secessionist sentiments, and when Louisiana joined the Confederacy he resigned from the US Army and made the characteristically dramatic gesture of enlisting in his state militia as a private soldier. On 1 March he was made a brigadier general. After Fort Sumter he was summoned to Richmond where Davis and Lee told him they expected the Northern army to march soon towards Manassas. They asked Beauregard to go there immediately and prepare the defence of the railway junction. Arriving on 1 June, he hurled himself into the task of surveying the area, organizing his forces to repel any enemy moves across Bull Run, demanding rapid reinforcement from Richmond, and setting up a spy network behind the Northern lines. One of his proposals to Davis and Lee, typically wild and histrionic, was

that he and his small army should advance to meet the enemy and 'sell our lives as dearly as practicable'. With Napoleonic hyperbole and disregard for the truth, he told civilians in the region: 'Abraham Lincoln, regardless of all moral, legal and constitutional restraints, has thrown his abolition hosts among you, who are murdering and imprisoning your citizens, confiscating and destroying your property, and committing other acts of violence and outrage too shocking and revolting to humanity to be enumerated.'

The other Southern commander was a very different personality. Joseph Eggleston Johnston was yet another Virginian of distinguished family background. They came originally from the Scottish Lowlands. His father (like Lee's) had fought in the War of Independence and later became a judge. At West Point, Jo Johnston showed an interest in academic as well as military matters – he was a keen student of French and astronomy. He fought, as an artillery officer, against the Seminole Indians under the command of General Scott, and later, as an engineering officer, against the Mexicans. He seemed to get himself wounded whenever he was in action. He was a lieutenant colonel when the Mexican War ended and had risen to be Quarter-Master Gen-

▲ *Jo Johnston was known as 'the gamecock' for his trim, erect, military bearing. Yet another Virginian, with a good army record, he was also a man of culture and courtesy. He got himself and his army on to the field at Bull Run in time to decide the issue and managed to work alongside Beauregard,* *though they quarrelled later on. A capable commander, he fought throughout the war. He died in 1891. (Anne S. K. Brown Mil. Coll., BUL)*

eral of the US Army, with the rank of brigadier general, by the beginning of 1861.

Once again his career ran closely parallel to that of Lee. He did not want Virginia to secede, but when it did he decided, after agonized reflection, to go with his state. Jefferson Davis welcomed him and promptly appointed him a major general, which meant that he out-ranked Beauregard.

Johnston could be a touchy and difficult subordinate, but he was an efficient, courteous and generous commander, much liked by his men. They called him 'the gamecock' in tribute to his trim, military figure and his jaunty manner.

For all that, Johnston was no hot-head. He had little time for those who thought Southerners had some sort of natural superiority as fighting men and that the war, in consequence, would be short and glorious. He knew professional soldiering and realized that his troops needed long and rigorous training before they would be ready for battle. When President Davis sent him to take charge of the army that was being formed in the Harpers Ferry region he set about drilling them hard.

On the Northern side the man who found himself facing Johnston was Major General Robert Patterson. He was a militia officer, not a regular. He had spent most of his life as a successful businessman with sugar and cotton plantations in the South, textile mills in the North and interests in railway and steamship companies. But he had fought in the War of 1812, becoming a colonel at the age of 20, and later as Winfield Scott's second-in-command on the march to Mexico City. Patterson's role at the First Battle of Bull Run was to be negative and yet highly influential. The outcome of the battle was determined, very largely, by his failure to occupy Johnston's full attention away from the main battlefield. After the defeat he was made the North's chief scapegoat. The judgement was not entirely fair; others were, in part, to blame. But Patterson was not the man for the job he was given. He was 69 years old. He had never had an independent command. He was a naturally cautious commander, always inclined to overestimate the enemy's strength. And, like the great majority of his soldiers, he was only serving on a three-month contract.

The Northern army that fought at First Bull Run was under the command of Irvin McDowell, an Ohio man. He was 42, just a few months younger than his antagonist Beauregard. In fact, they had been contemporaries at West Point, passing out in the class of 1838 – Beauregard second in a group of 45 cadets, McDowell 23rd. McDowell was not outstanding and did not seem particularly ambitious. He fought bravely in the Mexican War and was promoted to captain, but he never commanded so much as a company in action. He was a staff officer and stayed on Winfield Scott's staff after the war. By the beginning of 1861 he had risen one further rung up the promotion ladder to become a major.

So he was astonished in mid-May to be told

▲ Robert Patterson was not at Bull Run for the battle, and the defeat of the Northern side there is largely attributable to his failure to get himself and his army into the fight or, alternatively, to prevent Jo Johnston getting himself and his army into the fight. After the battle, Patterson was the prime scapegoat. He was neither entirely nor solely to blame, but it is undoubtedly true that his age (he was 69) and the extreme caution of his advance made it comparatively easy for Johnston to get away.

▲ Irvin McDowell was a decent, conscientious and capable commander with a wry turn of wit and a gargantuan appetite. His misfortune was to be promoted too fast. At the start of 1861 he was a major and had never even commanded a company in action. By July that year he was the general in command of the main army of the Union, charged with destroying the rebellion at its outset. His plan was sound. He fought hard. He made his worst mistakes on the field at the moment when it seemed as if the victory were his. (Anne S. K. Brown Mil. Coll., BUL)

that he had been appointed a brigadier general. Two weeks later, to his further amazement, he was given command of the Department of North-Eastern Virginia, which meant in effect that he would be in charge of the North's first attempt to subdue the Confederacy. The speed of his promotion upset many who had not been so favoured. Even Winfield Scott – an old friend – thought it had been excessive, and for some time there was a cooling-off in their relationship.

McDowell was a big, burly, square-jawed, bearded man, no drinker, but by all accounts a tremendous trencherman. He was an able officer and conscientious, but his manner was often abstracted and sometimes haughty, and this made him respected rather than liked by those subordinate to him. He was intelligent and articulate and had a cool wit. When the distinguished war correspondent of the London *Times*, William Howard Russell, arrived in Washington in early July, McDowell told him: 'I have made arrangements for the correspondents of our papers to take the field under certain regulations, and I have suggested to them that they should wear a white uniform to indicate the purity of their character.'

These were the four men who would run, as far as anyone did, the first real battle of the American Civil War. They were of varied qualities and abilities, but they all had one important thing in common: none of them had ever commanded any sizeable body of troops in battle. Even Winfield Scott had never commanded an army as large as those that were now being assembled. It was to be a formative factor.

THE OPPOSING ARMIES

The United States in 1860 was a profoundly unmilitary country. Its regular army was hardly more than 16,000 strong, most of them well away from the centres of population, manning scattered forts and arsenals or looking for signs of Indian trouble. It was a rare thing for a US citizen ever to see a soldier. This all changed very quickly in the spring of 1861.

Officers and Men

The outbreak of war was tumultuously welcomed on both sides. Young men rushed to enlist. Newspapers encouraged the frenzy. The long years of increasingly bitter dispute had built up into a great head of hatred and bigotry and ignorance, which now burst out into parades and public ceremonies, with much high-flown rhetoric, the waving of flags and the marching of men as the bands played on. It was a rich period for catchy marching tunes.

Most of the non-commissioned men in the US Army stayed loyal to the service of the Union, but

Left: an infantry private with primitive weaponry – an antiquated flintlock musket and a large Bowie knife. Flintlocks continued in use until 1862. Many volunteers brought their own Bowie knives with them but found little or no opportunity to use them in action, and they were rapidly discarded. Right, a private of the 4th Texas Infantry Regiment loads his smooth-bore percussion musket. He is hung about with a Bowie knife, bayonet, haversack and a tin canteen (water bottle) and, on his other

shoulder, a canvas sling to hold his cartridge box. Centre, a First Sergeant of the Louisiana Infantry was armed with a percussion rifle and an NCO's sword. He wears a 'havelock', a cloth flap to protect his neck from the sun. These were commonly worn in the first months of the Civil War but soon abandoned and used, more effectively, as coffee strainers. (Illustration by Ron Volstad)

they were – and remained – dotted about in small detachments in frontier regions. No more than 2,500 regular soldiers were in northern Virginia for the war's opening campaign. The result of Bull Run might have been very different had McDowell been able to deploy twice that number of trained men.

At the start of 1861 the officer corps of the United States army numbered just over 1,000. They were, for the most part, a highly professional body of officers, most of them the products of a four-year period of intensive study at West Point Military Academy in New York State. When the country split, more than half the officers whose homes were in the South resigned from the Union army and offered their services to the Confederacy. They included many of the best: Robert E. Lee and Jo Johnston and Beauregard; J.E.B. Stuart, the cavalry leader; Jubal Early and James Longstreet; and Thomas Jonathan (soon to be 'Stonewall') Jackson.

One of the peculiar cruelties of civil war is that it often divides families, turning blood brothers into enemies. The American Civil War also turned brother-officers into enemies. Many of them had trained, worked and fought together over many years. James Longstreet – a corps commander at First Bull Run, the son of a South Carolina planter, a tough man and little given to displays of emotion – was one of many who were deeply pained by the experience: 'It was a sad day', he wrote in his memoirs, 'when we took leave of life-time comrades and gave up a service of 20 years.'

The recruitment of volunteers, both North and South, was done regionally through the state militia system. It was the most simple and by far the best way; regional loyalties were still very strong. Some prominent local figure would be offered a captaincy and asked to form a company of volunteer infantrymen, between 60 and 80 men

ORDER OF BATTLE: THE SOUTHERN ARMY

I Corps
Commander
Brig. Gen. P. G. T. Beauregard

Assistant Adj. Gen.
Col. Thomas Jordan

2nd Brigade	4th Brigade	6th Brigade
Brig. Gen. R. S. Ewell	Brig. Gen. James Longstreet	Col. J. A. Early
Strength: 2,444	Strength: 3,528	Strength: 2,620

1st Brigade	3rd Brigade	5th Brigade
Brig. Gen. M. L. Bonham	Brig. Gen. D. R. Jones	Col. P. St. G Cocke
Strength: 4,961	Strength: 2,121	Strength: 3,276

Unbrigaded: 8th Louisiana (Col. H. B. Kelly), strength 846; Hampton's Legion (Col. Wade Hampton), strength 6!

Cavalry: Harrison's Battalion (Maj. Julian Harrison), strength 209; 30th Virginia Cavalry (Col. R. C. W. Radford), strength 300; plus ten independent companies, with a total strength of 583.

II Corps
Commander
Gen. J. E. Johnston

Assistant Adj. Gen.
Brig. Gen. E. K. Smith

1st Brigade	2nd Brigade	3rd Brigade	4th Brigade
Brig. Gen. T. J. Jackson	Col. F. S. Bartow	Brig. Gen. B. E. Bee	Brig. Gen. E. K. Smith
Strength: 2,151	Strength: 2,546	Strength: 2,790	Strength: 2,262

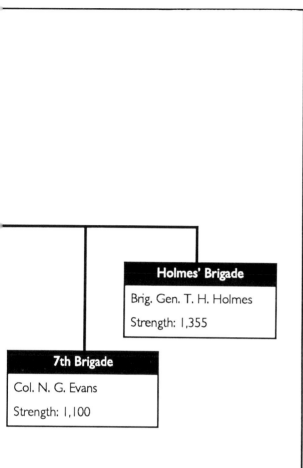

Holmes' Brigade

Brig. Gen. T. H. Holmes

Strength: 1,355

7th Brigade

Col. N. G. Evans

Strength: 1,100

Unbrigaded:
6th North Carolina Infantry (Col. C. F. Fisher),
strength 600; Beckham's Virginia Battalion
(Lt. R. F. Beckham).

Cavalry:
"Jeb" Stuart's men of the 1st Virginia.
There were 334 of them.

all told. He would chose two friends or acquaintances as his lieutenants, and the three of them together would then find their recruits. Generally speaking, a company would be made up of young men who had been neighbours all their lives, who had grown up together and knew each other's strengths and weaknesses. It made for *espirit de corps* but not always for good discipline.

In both armies, in theory, ten companies comprised one regiment. This would be commanded by a lieutenant colonel, who would have a small headquarters staff. The men of a regiment were usually all from the same state. In ideal circumstances a regiment meant about 1,000 men, but this number was rarely approached in practice. In very approximate terms, four or five regiments were said to form a brigade, which would be commanded by a full colonel or a brigadier general. In even more approximate terms, three or four brigades made up a division. One or more divisions could form a corps.

The key operational unit was the brigade, in theory between 4,000 and 5,000 men, in practice usually much fewer than that.

In some respects, the quality of the recruits was superb. They were young men, most of whom had grown up with enough to eat and plenty of hard physical work in the fresh air. Many of them had led tough and spartan lives. They were used to roughing it. Many were also well-used to handling weapons – shotguns, hunting rifles and pistols. They were highly motivated too. Most of them, on both sides, sincerely believed in the justice of their cause. They signed on for a wide variety of motives: because they liked fighting and did not want to miss 'the big one'; because all their friends were going; to see something of the world (most of them had never travelled outside their immediate locality); because they thought it would be exciting and different and probably fun and possibly glorious and, anyway, over quite soon. Both North and South set a minimum age limit of 18, but under-age lads on both sides wanted to join in. Many had been brought up to speak the truth so they wrote '18' on a slip of paper and put it inside one of their shoes so that when the inevitable question was asked they could honestly reply; 'I am over 18'.

They were raw material for the making of superb infantrymen. The only trouble was that they were without military training and experience of any kind, and they had, on the whole, a sturdy aversion to the kind of discipline that army life traditionally demands. This was true of the new officers as well as the men. They resented the intrusion into their lives of West Pointers with their rigid attitudes to the way things should be done, their insistence on obedience, the harsh punishments they inflicted when their orders were defied or ignored.

The streak of individualism was even stronger in the young American men in those days than it is now. They had been brought up to admire and emulate the pioneer virtues, respect for personal freedom, self-reliance, the importance of being 'your own man'. It was considered unmanly to let yourself be pushed around by someone else, to give automatic and unquestioning obedience. And these ingrained attitudes were not going to be changed the moment a man volunteered for a short spell in the army. The European armies of the twentieth century have more than once been astonished by the relaxed American way of running an army, their democratic approach to decision-making. It was even more marked in 1861, and it made things more difficult for those in command on both sides.

Uniforms

Recruitment on both sides was based on the local militia system, and over the preceding years these forces had enjoyed much local autonomy. Many had sought to attract men to their ranks by offering a lively social life, much parading about on festive

▼ *The American Civil War was the first to produce a full pictorial record, in photographs and sketches, but photography was in its early stages and could not cope with men in movement. It gave much scope to the artists. Frank Vitzetelli portrayed a regiment of New York*

Zouaves parading along Broadway on their way to Washington and then Bull Run. Before he went to America, Vitzetelli had covered Garibaldi's campaigns in Sicily and Italy for the Illustrated London News. *(Illustrated London News, 22 June 1861)*

▲*A sergeant of the 7th New York State Militia, one of the earliest militia regiments to go to Washington and join the Army of the Potomac.*

Many Northern units wore grey uniforms at that time, which helped to increase the confusion at First Bull Run. (Illustration by Michael Youens)

▲*A regular army private of the 6th US Infantry Regiment. Had McDowell had more such trained and experienced men at Bull Run the result might well*

have been very different. (Illustration by Michael Youens)

occasions and – above all else – by the splendour of their uniforms. As a result, a colourful and exotic variety of uniforms, reflecting foreign or historical influences, had been adopted.

Some based their designs on the costumes worn by the American colonists in the War of Independence. Others looked across the Atlantic for their models. The 39th New York Infantry, impressed by the success of the Italian freedom fighters under Garibaldi, affected the style of the *bersaglieri* sharp-shooters, including hats with flamboyant plumes. The 79th New York, recruited largely from Scottish immigrants, modelled themselves on the Cameron Highlanders with a dress uniform of kilts, sporran, silver-buckled shoes and Glengarry caps, though they changed into trousers and boots for Bull Run. But it was the French influence that predominated, North and South. If the strategic skills of the first Napoleon prevailed in West Point's battle training, it was the sartorial extravagances of Napoleon III's army that prevailed in the matter of dress, especially those of his Algerian soldiers, the Zouaves. Many militia units, on both sides, fitted themselves out with baggy trousers in bright colours (usually red), yellow or white gaiters and short blue jackets, fancifully embroidered. The men wore a red *fez* with a long tassel; the officers wore *kepis*.

In the spring of 1861, when the mass recruitment drives had been launched, each government tried to impose some measure of uniformity on its army's appearance: the North chose blue as its distinctive colour; the South opted for grey. In this way, it was hoped, in the smoky confusion of battle their soldiers would have some way of distinguishing friend from foe. Unfortunately neither

▶ *Vitzetelli's impression of 'Colonel Wilson's boys' in camp on Staten Island. One of the things the volunteers had to get used to once they were in the army was the amount of sheer 'hanging about' and waiting that military service involves. It led to a great deal of drunkenness and brawling. (Illustrated London News, 29 June 1861)*

◀ *Vitzetelli's portraits of two members, an officer and a private, of Colonel Elmer E. Ellsworth's 11th New York Fire Zouaves (most of them had been in the city's fire brigade). Colonel Ellsworth did not get to Bull Run. He was killed in a minor skirmish at the outset of the campaign, becoming one of the first casualties of the Civil War. The 11th New York went on to face some of the fiercest fighting on the summit of Henry Hill. (Illustrated London News, 15 June 1861)*

side was able to implement its orders immediately, so both armies marched to Bull Run displaying an astonishing mixture of uniforms. Some Southern units and many of their senior commanders were dressed in blue, while several Northern regiments wore grey tunics and trousers. It was to cost lives and affect the course of the battle at important moments.

Weapons

First Bull Run was primarily an infantry encounter, and the best infantryman's weapon was the 1855 version of the Springfield rifle-musket. Its overall length was four feet eight inches, and it weighed just over nine pounds. It was a muzzle-loader firing a .58 calibre bullet, just over half an inch in diameter. Muzzle-loading was a complicated procedure, but tests conducted in 1860 showed that a trained man could load and fire the rifle ten times in five minutes, putting six of his bullets into a two-foot square target at a distance of 100 yards. At 300 yards' range he put all ten bullets into a target that was two and a half feet

square. Manufactured in the armoury at Springfield, Massachusetts, this was by far the best infantry weapon available in 1861. It meant that attackers could no longer get to within 150 yards of the enemy line, then form up and charge, confident that the defenders would have time to fire no more than one volley before they were among them with the bayonet.

The Springfield 1855 was used by both sides at Bull Run. The Confederates got many when they seized the Federal arsenals within their territories. But neither side had anything like enough to arm all their men with them, and the rest had to make do with a variety of more ancient weapons – smooth-bore muskets, like today's shotguns, which were unlikely to hit a man at anything over 200 yards, and the even more antiquated flintlocks. The only effective use for guns like this was a mass volley at short range.

The artillery had long been something of a Cinderella in both the Union army and the state militias. The equipment was expensive; the gunner's work was noisy and dirty, hard and dangerous; it called for some technical skill and

◀ *Vitzetelli makes the camp of the 2nd New York Regiment look clean, well-ordered and busy. Many of the regimental camps, in the early days of the war, were not like that.* (Illustrated London News, *29 June 1861*)

much rigorous drill. To be a gunner was more demanding than to be an infantryman and was nothing like as glamorous as being a cavalryman. Perhaps for these reasons the artillery tended to attract to its ranks men of a more serious and dedicated disposition and, once in, they quickly learned to take great pride in their work. Although not many guns were taken to Bull Run – the North had 55 altogether, the South 49 – the artillery played an important role.

There was a great variety of guns, ranging from six-pounders to one 30-pounder. Most of them were smooth-bores, but some had rifled barrels, which gave greater range and accuracy. All were muzzle-loaders. The most popular was the 12-pounder 1857 Model, generally known as the 'Napoleon'. Most of these were smooth-bores, capable of hurling their missiles farther than a mile but with an effective range of about 1,500 yards. The gunner had a selection of missiles: solid iron balls weighing over 12 pounds that flew at 1,440 feet per second to cut a terrible swathe through enemy ranks; shells filled with powder that exploded on impact; grapeshot and canister, which exploded into showers of metal fragments. With a full and trained crew, a sergeant (or corporal) and seven gunners, the 12-pounder could be fired twice a minute. In ideal circumstances, a battery would comprise six guns and their supporting ammunition wagons (caissons), requiring a total of 72 horses.

The guns were influential at Bull Run chiefly because most of them were manned by regular soldiers, fully trained and animated by high professional zeal. Nine of the Northern batteries came from the regular Union army. On the Southern side many of the artillery officers were West Point men, and many more had learned their craft at Virginia Military Institute under the expert gunner and strict instructor, Major T. J. Jackson.

The Cavalry

In cavalry, the Southern forces had a marked advantage. At the end of 1860 the US army included only five regiments of cavalry (something over 1,000 mounted men to each regiment), and these were scattered about the frontier regions to the west in small units, keeping an eye on the Indians. When the Confederacy was formed, four of the five regular colonels resigned to join the South. The Northern commanders made no effort to get their cavalry units back to the Washington area in force, nor – when the call went out for volunteers – did they ask for cavalrymen. They assumed that the war would be quickly over and that it would be won by infantrymen with a little

▼State uniforms of the South. Left, a staff captain from South Carolina. Centre, a corporal of the Alabama Volunteer Corps. Right, a private in the 11th Mississippi Infantry Regiment, which was part of General Bee's 3rd Brigade at First Bull Run. (Illustrated by Ron Volstad)

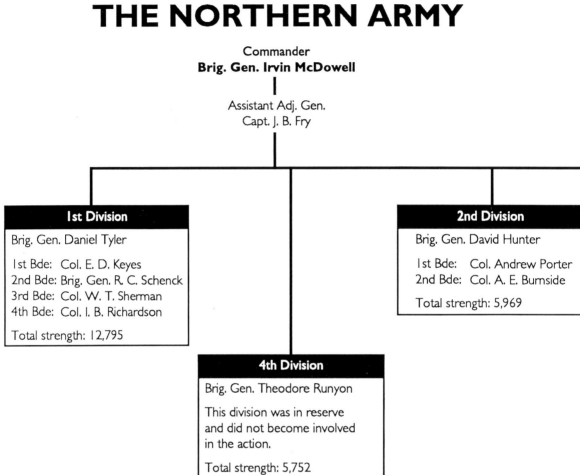

ORDER OF BATTLE:
THE NORTHERN ARMY

Commander
Brig. Gen. Irvin McDowell

Assistant Adj. Gen.
Capt. J. B. Fry

1st Division

Brig. Gen. Daniel Tyler

1st Bde: Col. E. D. Keyes
2nd Bde: Brig. Gen. R. C. Schenck
3rd Bde: Col. W. T. Sherman
4th Bde: Col. I. B. Richardson

Total strength: 12,795

2nd Division

Brig. Gen. David Hunter

1st Bde: Col. Andrew Porter
2nd Bde: Col. A. E. Burnside

Total strength: 5,969

4th Division

Brig. Gen. Theodore Runyon

This division was in reserve
and did not become involved
in the action.

Total strength: 5,752

There was also one battalion (seven companies) of cavalry, commanded by Maj. I. N. Palmer.
They marched with Col. Porter's brigade of the 2nd Division.

The North had a marginal numerical advantage. McDowell commanded some 38,000 men, though many were not engaged in the battle. The forces of Beauregard and Johnston totaled 35,000, and many of these, too, saw little or no fighting. The North had a few more guns. The South had more and better cavalry.

help from the gunners. There was no need, it was felt, to go to the considerable expense that cavalry involved. The thinking was wrong, as subsequent developments in the Civil War were to prove, but it meant that McDowell marched to Bull Run with only 500 horsemen under his command – and disposed them in such a way as to ensure that they could be of little use. There was no mounted reconnaissance screen in front of his advancing troops; no protection of the exposed flanks; no information-gathering from enemy territory; no chance of ever assembling a mobile strike force that might thrust a way through the Southern defensive lines.

3rd Division

Brig. Gen. S. P. Heintzelman

1st Bde: Brig. Gen. W. B. Franklin
2nd Bde: Brig. Gen. O. B. Willcox
3rd Bde: Brig. Gen. O. O. Howard

Total strength: 7,232

5th Division

Brig. Gen. D. S. Miles

1st Bde: Col. Louis Blenker
2nd Bde: Col. T. A. Davies

Total strength: 6,173

Horsemanship was more highly regarded in the rural and aristocratic South. It formed a vital part in the upbringing of every young gentleman. The image of the dashing *beau sabreur* was a compelling one. As a result, the Southern forces at First Bull Run included more than 3,000 mounted men organized into seven separate companies and two regiments. Many of them had fine mounts. They were armed with carbines, revolvers and sabres. One regiment, the First Virginia Cavalry commanded by the ebullient J.E.B. Stuart, was to play a key role at the turning-point of the battle.

Intelligence

Civil wars are complicated. There were people in the Southern states who hated slavery as much as any Northerner, who opposed secession and hoped for an early Northern victory. A few of them worked clandestinely to further the Union cause, sabotaging the military where they could, getting information to the Northern commanders. Support for the Southern cause in the Northern states was even greater. Many believed the war was a terrible mistake, that it had been brought about by anti-slavery intolerance, and that if the slave states wanted to go their own way, they should be allowed to do so in peace. In some places, in Missouri, for example, and in the city of Baltimore,

▼*A group of young Virginians who responded immediately to the state's call for one-year's service in the army. In many ways they were ideal recruits –* *young, strong and keen – but it was to prove difficult, on both sides, to imbue them with proper notions of military discipline.*

pro-South feeling was intense. It was very strong, too, in the national capital, Washington. As a result, nothing could be kept secret from the enemy for long. Troop movements of any size were noted and reported. There were Southern sympathizers with friends in very high places, and Lincoln and his top advisers soon had to accept the fact that their plans would be known to the enemy leaders within days. There was no simple way of recognizing the spies. It was impossible to police the borders effectively.

Universal Inexperience

The overriding fact about the First Battle of Bull Run is that neither side was anything like ready for it. The generals on both sides had no experience of commanding even moderately large bodies of soldiers in battle. Some had never had an independent command of any size. And the great majority of the soldiers, again on both sides, had no experience of war and had received the most perfunctory training. There were some units that had not even been taught how to load and fire their muskets. None had been properly drilled in the complex manoeuvres required to get regiments or brigades into the necessary battle formations. Few

▲ *In the early hours of the morning of 24 May 1861, Winfield Scott sent strong contingents of his army, mostly New York volunteers, out of Washington and across the Long Bridge over the Potomac and into Virginia, to seize the towns of Alexandria and Arlington. There was no resistance, though Colonel Ellsworth was killed in Alexandria – shot by an angry householder when he went on to his roof to haul down the rebel flag. (From* Harper's Weekly; *Anne S.K. Brown Coll. BUL)*

had been instilled with any real sense of military discipline.

The Times' correspondent William Howard Russell was shocked by what he found when he toured McDowell's camps in early July. He was a neutral observer and an expert one; he had seen the professional armies of Europe in action, the Prussians in Schleswig-Holstein, the French and the British in the Crimea, the British again in the suppression of the Indian mutineers. The camps, he wrote in his diary, were dirty. Discipline was criminally lax. Officers as well as men were incapable of even company drill movements. General McDowell could find no adequate map of the area he was soon to invade and had a completely inadequate staff: 'They have no cavalry, only a few scarecrow men, who would dissolve partnership with their steeds at the first serious

▼*Full-dress infantry in the Northern army, 1861. Left to right, a first lieutenant, colonel and sergeant-major. (Illustration by Ron Volstad)*

combined movement . . . they have no carriage for reserve ammunition; the commissariat drivers are civilians, under little or no control; the officers are unsoldierly-looking men; the camps are dirty to excess; the men are dressed in all sorts of uniforms; and, from what I hear, I doubt if any of these regiments have ever performed a brigade evolution together or if any of the officers know what it is to deploy a brigade from column into line. They are mostly three months' men whose time is nearly up.'

Apart from the description of the cavalry, perhaps, and the matter of the three months' term of service, much the same account might have been made of the Southern forces.

Bruce Catton, the distinguished American historian of the Civil War, wrote: 'There is nothing in American military history quite like the story of Bull Run. It was the momentous fight of the amateurs, the battle where everything went wrong,

▲ In the early months of the Civil War, both sides had difficulty in imposing march discipline. Their volunteer recruits saw no good reason why they should not stop and rest when they felt like it or forage about for food and drink.

▶ Thomas Jonathan Jackson of Virginia was a young colonel when the Civil War began. But he was a general in command of a brigade at First Bull Run, and it was on the summit slopes of Henry Hill that he won the nickname 'Stonewall'. More than any of the other commanders on the field that day, he distinguished himself and won great respect and fame. After Bull Run, he continued to fight hard and skilfully – at Antietam, in the Shenandoah Valley, at Fredericksburg – but he was severely wounded at Chancellorsville in 1863 and died soon after. (Photograph by Minnes, Fredericksburg, 1863)*

the great day of awakening for the whole nation, North and South together. It marked the end of the 90-day militia, and it also ended the rosy time in which men could dream that the war would be short, glorious and bloodless. After Bull Run the nation got down to business.'

THE ROAD TO BULL RUN

By June 1861 there were four armies in the process of formation in North-East Virginia and a general recognition that it was in this region that the war's first major encounter would take place. McDowell was creating his army in and around Washington while Beauregard did the same and prepared his defences beyond the Bull Run river. Just over 30 miles to the north-west meanwhile, in the Shenandoah Valley beyond the Blue Ridge Mountains, the rather smaller armies of Robert Patterson and Jo Johnston were sparring with each other.

The village of Harpers Ferry, at the junction of the Rivers Potomac and Shenandoah, had been abandoned by the Northern forces in mid-April. By the end of the month the region was under the control of a small Virginian force commanded by Colonel Thomas J. Jackson.

Jackson was a young man, in his mid-thirties,

but already an experienced officer. Of mixed Scottish and Irish descent, he was a Virginian by birth and loyalty. He had graduated from West Point, fought as an artillery lieutenant in the Mexican War, and later had become a teacher of military science and mathematics. More important than this, he was a man of powerful character, serious and strong-minded. He was deeply Christian: 'He lives by the New Testament and fights by the Old', someone said of him. His regard for the Bible was almost matched by his regard for army regulations and military discipline. He was one of those officers whose men dislike him initially because of his stern rule but who soon comes to command respect and affection for his fairness and integrity and his air of knowing exactly what he is about.

Jackson's force expanded rapidly as the volunteers arrived, and when their number reached some 9,000 a more senior officer, Brigadier General Joseph E. Johnston, was sent to take over. He formed the army into four brigades and gave Jackson command of the First Brigade, composed of four (later five) Virginia regiments.

Johnston had other impressive men under his command. One of them was the charismatic young cavalry leader, James Ewell Brown Stuart. In many ways Stuart was the epitome of the romantic notion of a cavalry leader – handsome, strong, extrovert in manner, flamboyant in appearance, exuding confidence and cheerfulness, full of energy and courage. Johnston called him a 'yellow jacket' which was a type of hornet. It is a tribute to 'Jeb' Stuart's qualities that he won the respect of the Presbyterian Jackson, despite the disparity in their characters.

Another junior officer who was to distinguish himself at Bull Run and earn high promotion was Captain John D. Imboden of the artillery. In his account *Incidents of the First Bull Run* Imboden said

Northern Virginia and the opposing armies, mid-June 1861

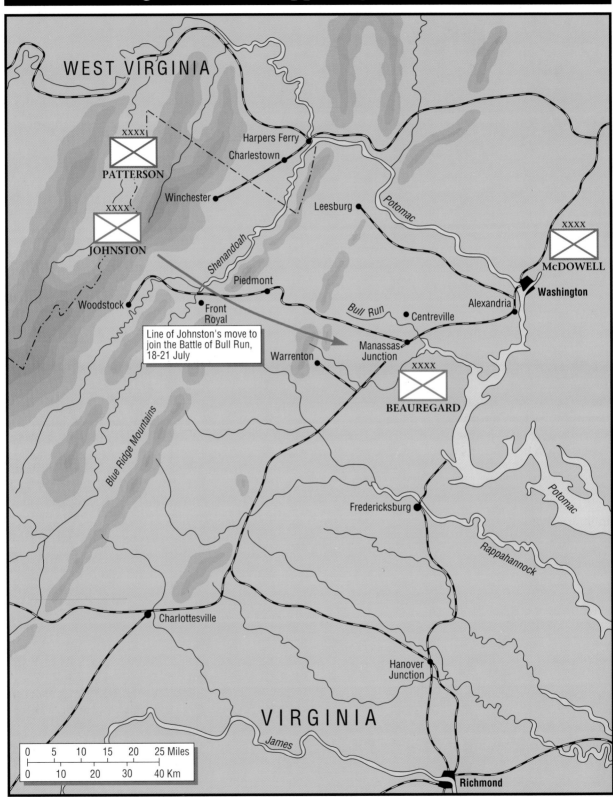

WEST VIRGINIA

XXXX
PATTERSON

Harpers Ferry
Charlestown

Winchester

XXXX
JOHNSTON

Leesburg

Potomac

XXXX
McDOWELL

Washington

Piedmont

Shenandoah

Woodstock

Front
Royal

Bull Run

Centreville

Alexandria

Line of Johnston's move to
join the Battle of Bull Run,
18-21 July

Warrenton

Manassas
Junction

XXXX
BEAUREGARD

Blue Ridge Mountains

Fredericksburg

Potomac

Rappahannock

Charlottesville

Hanover
Junction

VIRGINIA

James

0   5   10   15   20   25 Miles

0   10   20   30   40 Km

Richmond

that Johnston, in these weeks before the battle, 'was ceaseless in his labours to improve the efficiency of his little army'. Johnston had Jackson's belief in the need for discipline and drill, and when circumstances allowed he carried on with Jackson's programme of intensive training. Luckily, he was given plenty of time. The commander he faced was the elderly Robert Patterson.

Patterson was beset with troubles, some of them real, some imaginary. Like most of his soldiers, he had only signed on for three months. Unlike most of them, he knew about war, enough at least to know that they were unfit for battle, inadequately equipped and insufficiently trained. He was not the man to fill them with confidence. He suffered under the constant delusion that the enemy forces facing him were much stronger than his own. This encouraged his natural caution, which was further stimulated by the orders he received from Winfield Scott in Washington. Advance slowly, he was told, and with great care; risk no reverses; make no aggressive moves unless success is certain.

In early June, Johnston decided that his positions around Harpers Ferry were scarcely defensible and of no strategic importance anyway, so he withdrew his forces to the Winchester area. He was better-placed here to deal with attacks either from the north or the west, and also, should the call come, to hurry to support Beauregard. Patterson moved towards Harpers Ferry with infinite caution. Even when he finally arrived there and found the enemy gone, he was suspicious. He was being lured, he thought, into a cunning trap. The tentative nature of his advance was increased in mid-June when Winfield Scott, without any apparent evidence, decided that Washington was in imminent danger and ordered Patterson to dispatch his only really reliable units, the regular contingents, to save the capital immediately.

Public opinion in the North, which had been so confident, was growing impatient. There was an increasing demand for decisive action of some kind. The newspapers, as usual, reflected and magnified the popular feeling. The most influential of them, the *New York Tribune*, under its eccentric and excitable editor Horace Greeley, led the chorus with its repeated headline cry 'Forward

▲*James Ewell Brown Stuart, universally known as 'Jeb', was a cavalry leader of dash and distinction who made a considerable contribution to the Southern victory at First Bull Run – first by* *effectively fooling Patterson in the Shenandoah Valley, then by his charges in and around Henry Hill at the turning-point of the battle. (Photograph by George E. Cook)*

to Richmond'.

President Lincoln and his top advisers felt the weight of all this pressure and were also aware that their troops' three-month term of service would begin to expire in mid-July.

Northern Plans

On 29 June the President held a meeting of his ministers and top military advisers in the White House. Winfield Scott, asked for his advice, argued against giving in to the general clamour. He was in favour of further training and preparation throughout the summer to be followed in the autumn by an attack in force down the Mississippi Valley to reach the sea and split the Confederacy in two. In this way, together with a blockade by the Union navy, the hardline secessionist states would be cut off from all help. It was called the 'Anaconda Plan', after the South American snake that squeezes its victims to death. In the event, three years later, the North was to win the war by some such method; but the idea was altogether too long-term for Northern sentiment in June 1861. Scott's ideas were dismissed with little discussion. The old general gave way without a struggle, and the meeting went on to consider the plans McDowell had already drawn up for an attack on Manassas Junction.

McDowell had made these plans a few days earlier at Scott's request. He now stuck a map on the wall and expounded them. He reckoned the enemy strength behind Bull Run at about 25,000 and, assuming that Patterson would keep Johnston fully occupied in the Shenandoah Valley, he thought they might have another 10,000 men in the field by the time of the battle. The enemy was expecting them and had been preparing his defences. McDowell proposed to advance with a force of some 30,000 men, followed by a reserve of 10,000. He would not attack frontally but hoped to work round the eastern flank of the enemy, then strike westwards along the line of the Orange and Alexandria Railroad to cut Beauregard off from his supply line from Richmond.

▼*Frank Vitzetelli was in Washington in the early summer of 1861 to observe and sketch the build-up of the Northern army. Here President Lincoln with members of his Cabinet and General Winfield Scott (seated) watch a parade of volunteer soldiers shortly before the Battle of Bull Run.* (Illustrated London News)

It was a simple and sensible plan, and no one present had anything better to suggest. McDowell stressed the importance of the coming battle and added: 'I think it of great consequence that, as for the most part our regiments are exceedingly raw and the best of them, with few exceptions, not over steady in line, they be organized into as many small fixed brigades as the number of regular colonels will admit . . . so that the men may have as fair a chance as the nature of things and the comparative inexperience of most will allow.'

Someone asked when the march to Manassas would start; Scott, without consulting McDowell, said it would begin in one week's time.

At some point, either towards the close of this meeting or immediately after it, McDowell repeated his concern about the 'green-ness' of his troops. The reply – sometimes attributed to Lincoln, sometimes to Scott – was: 'You are green, it is true, but they are green also.'

Scott's deadline for the start of the march proved impossible to meet. There was a shortage of transport wagons, horses and mules. More recruits were still on the way. McDowell complained: 'I had no opportunity to test my machinery, to move it around and see whether it would work smoothly or not.' Finally, on 15 July he called his corps commanders together and told them they would march next day. His field order warned them to proceed with caution and to remember the variety of uniforms and make sure their men did not fire on each other.

They set off on the afternoon of the next day, each man carrying three days' rations in his haversack.

Southern Preparations

Beauregard had known for weeks that they would soon be coming, and he received confirmation that they were on the way before 9 o'clock that night. A coded message was handed to him. It came from a leader of Washington society with friends in high places and intense sympathy for the Southern cause, Mrs. Rose O'Neal Greenhow. The note said: 'Order issued for McDowell to march upon Manassas tonight.' Immediately Beauregard sent orders to his outposts to fall back quietly as McDowell's men approached. Then he asked President Davis to alert Johnston and get him to start transferring his army to Manassas.

In the late afternoon of 17 July, Johnston received a telegram from Beauregard: 'War Department has ordered you to join me. Do so immediately, if possible, and we will crush the enemy.' The order from the War Department in Richmond arrived in the early hours of the next morning. Johnston summoned his brigade commanders and organized the move. Jackson's Brigade, which already had a reputation for fast marching, would go first. The men would not be told what was happening until well clear of the area so that word would not reach Patterson. One after the other, the brigades would make for the railway at Piedmont. An officer rode ahead to alert the railway authorities and arrange for trains to ferry the infantrymen the 34 miles to Manassas Junction. Artillery and cavalry would have to get there under their own steam.

When the march began the men were downhearted, believing this was another strategic withdrawal. Then they were halted and Johnston's order was read out, making it clear they were on their way to a big battle. 'The soldiers rent the air with shouts of joy', Jackson reported, 'and all was eagerness and animation.' The first men reached Manassas at 4 p.m. on Friday 19 July.

'Jeb' Stuart and his cavalry were given the job of screening the army's departure from Patterson, and in this they were completely successful. For reasons known only to himself, Patterson had moved his army to the area of Charlestown, more than 20 miles from Winchester. He had been reinforced with more volunteers, bringing the number of men under his command to about 17,000, but he persisted in his belief that Johnston was much stronger than that. He was, furthermore, getting confused and even contradictory orders from Winfield Scott. He was having to plead with the three-months' men, whose term of service was amost up, to stay a few days longer. Everything conspired to encourage his natural caution. But right until the last moment, and beyond it – when Johnston's brigades were steaming towards Bull Run – Patterson still believed he was holding Johnston in the Shenandoah Valley.

THE AFFAIR AT BLACKBURN'S FORD

McDowell's orders for the march from Washington towards Bull Run were clear and sensible, and at first all went well, though slowly. Beauregard had told his foremost units to observe the enemy columns closely but to pull back, offering no resistance. When the tracks ran through woodland, as they often did, they felled trees to delay the Nothern advance a little.

The weather was hot and sultry. Many of the advancing men, who had overloaded themselves, began to shed clothing and equipment they thought unnecessary. Some suffered from sunstroke, all from thirst. The colonel of the Third Brigade of the First Division, who had only been given that command a fortnight before, was shocked at his men's behaviour: 'The march demonstrated little save the general laxity of discipline; for with all my personal efforts, I could not prevent the men from straggling for water, blackberries, or anything on the way they fancied.' This was William Tecumseh Sherman, whose original approach to warfare was later to make a clinching impact on the course of the Civil War and influence subsequent military thinking. The historian, Sir Basil Liddell Hart, called Sherman 'the first modern strategist' for his perception that wars could be won by striking at the enemy's economic power base and undermining his morale, rather than by fighting great and bloody battles. But in July 1861 this part of Sherman's career was still to come. Sherman was just turned 40. An Ohio man, he went to West Point, was commissioned into the artillery, saw action against the Seminole Indians and the Mexicans, then resigned from the army to try his luck in business. In April 1861 he volunteered for three years' service and was made a colonel. In appearance and manner he was like many Americans of that time – tall and loose-limbed; careless of dress and restless; a cigar chain-smoker with considerable contempt for con-

ventional thinking and a powerful, picturesque way of stating his views. He also had great energy and courage, a quick and acute intelligence. He took his soldiering seriously. He believed in marching light. On his way to Bull Run he wrote to his wife, thanking her for her letters and adding tactlessly: 'As I read them I will tear them up, for every ounce on a march tells.'

▼*William Tecumseh Sherman was just 40 years old and the colonel commanding the 3rd Brigade of the 1st Division of the North's army at Bull Run. He showed initiative by finding a way across the river to get his men into the thick of the action, but after that did nothing to* *mark himself out as a man with a great military future. After Bull Run he briefly thought his army career was over, but he survived and later emerged to become one of the most innovative and important of the war's leaders. (Anne S. K. Brown Mil. Coll., BUL)*

▲ *A corporal of the 1st Virginia Regiment, which was hotly engaged in the affair at Blackburn's Ford, but – as part of General Longstreet's 4th Brigade – played virtually no part in the main Bull Run battle.*

(Illustration by Michael Youens)

▲ *Colonel Ambrose Burnside raised the First Rhode Island Infantry Regiment and became their colonel. They played an active part in the First Battle of Bull Run under his brigade command. He designed their uniform – this is a corporal – which included a red woollen blanket and, for some of the men, carbines designed by Burnside himself. (Illustration by Michael Youens)*

McDowell's army pushed forward much more slowly than he and his senior commanders would have liked, though in reasonable order. There was some looting and foraging, but it was firmly dealt with. McDowell still hoped to be able to follow his original plan – to feint a frontal attack across Bull Run while a strong force marched round to the east of the enemy defences to drive in behind him on the line of the Orange and Alexandria Railroad. For the task of turning the enemy line he looked to his Third Division, commanded by Colonel Samuel P. Heintzelman. Heintzelman had been an army officer for 35 years, showing courage in action against both Indians and Mexicans. On 18

July, McDowell and Heintzelman rode out to reconnoitre the ground the Third Division would have to cover to outflank Beauregard's main force. What they saw was disappointing: 'The roads', McDowell found, 'were too narrow and crooked for so large a body to move over, and the distance around too great to admit of it with any safety. We would become entangled and our carriages would block up the way.' McDowell would have to re-think his next moves.

In the meantime he had to take the village of Centreville and push on beyond towards the River Bull Run, sounding out the enemy's strength. This job he gave to his strongest division, the First, with four brigades and a total strength of more than 12,000 men, under the command of Brigadier General Daniel Tyler.

Tyler's Attack

Tyler was 62. He had been a soldier for the first half of his career, then a successful businessman. Although he had seen no action, he had a military manner. And he was ambitious – perhaps he was

◀ *Frank Vizetelli allowed himself a good measure of artistic and journalistic licence. It is not likely that he got ahead of McDowell's vanguard on the march to Fairfax (en route for Centreville), but he none the less sent his magazine this lively impression of South Carolina pickets pulling back and setting up obstacles to delay the enemy's advance.* (Illustrated London News)

◀ *This sketch by Vizetelli is entirely imaginary. In fact, the little town of Fairfax was taken without a shot being fired. McDowell expected stiff resistance here, but when Colonel Burnside's brigade arrived it was to find that the Southern forces had withdrawn.* (Illustrated London News, 22 June 1861)

▲ *Brigadier General Daniel Tyler, commander of the North's 1st Division, was highly ambitious and resented taking orders from McDowell. He did much to harm the North's chances at Bull Run. In the preliminary probing skirmish – the affair at Blackburn's Ford on July 18 – he exceeded his* orders and was so badly mauled that the morale of the whole army was affected. At Bull Run itself he went to the opposite extreme and moved with such caution that half his Division never got involved in the key struggle. (Anne S. K. Brown Mil. Coll., BUL)

▲ *James Longstreet, commander of Beauregard's 4th Brigade, fought a capable action at Blackburn's Ford to repulse Tyler's attack on 18 July. But on the day of the Bull Run battle, although Longstreet's men were intended to be part of the attack on Centreville and though* they crossed and re-crossed the river more than once, they saw little action. (Anne S. K. Brown Mil. Coll., BUL)

one of the several officers who were offended when McDowell was promoted over their heads in May. Certainly, he had no great liking or respect for McDowell.

McDowell was clear in the orders he gave Tyler: 'Observe well the roads to Bull Run and to Warrenton,' he said. 'Do not bring on an engagement, but keep up the impression that we are moving on Manassas.'

The enemy went on falling back before him as Tyler pushed on through Centreville and beyond until he came to the crest of a hill and looked down on a well-wooded landscape and the Bull Run. There were two fords across the river immediately ahead, Mitchell's and Blackburn's. On the far side he could see some enemy soldiers. He called up two big rifled guns, 20-pounders, and got them to fire a few shots. There was a brief response, but

the Southern guns were smooth-bore and lacked the range.

Beauregard's line of defence was some six miles in length, following the river from Union Mills Ford on his right to the Stone Bridge on his left. The brigade in position behind Blackburn's Ford was that of Brigadier General James Longstreet, a cool and capable officer. He had had time to prepare, and most of his men were well-concealed. He held his fire.

Tyler had been surprised by the ease of his advance so far. With a little vigorous pushing, he felt, he might march on to Manassas Junction and seize the day's glory, putting one over on McDowell in the process. He either forgot, or chose to ignore, McDowell's order that he should do nothing to bring on an engagement. He called up more guns to join him on the hilltop, then ordered two companies of the Fourth Brigade to advance towards the river.

These were men of the First Massachusetts Regiment, led by Lieutenant Colonel George D. Wells. As they moved forward, they came under scattered fire from retreating skirmishers. In a wood one of the companies, commanded by Lieutenant W. H. B. Smith, ran into a group of Southerners who were in grey uniforms similar to their own. 'Who are you?', the Southerners called. 'Massachusetts men,' they replied. There was an immediate volley and Lieutenant Smith was killed. The confusion of uniforms was to cause more trouble in the next four days.

The Massachusetts men emerged on to clearer ground just above Blackburn's Ford to find themselves under heavy fire from three sides and from an enemy they could not see. 'We were in the thick of it full 15 minutes,' Colonel Wells said, 'the balls humming like a bee-hive.' He organized his men, however, and they returned the enemy fire with sufficient accuracy to cause consternation among some of the raw Southern soldiers. Longstreet later wrote in his *Memoirs*: 'The first pouring-down volleys were most startling to the new troops. Part of my line broke and started at a run. To stop the alarm I rode with sabre in hand for the leading files, determined to give them all that was in the sword and my horse's heels, or stop the break. They seemed to see as much danger in their rear as in front, and soon turned . . .'

Colonel Wells retreated to the top of the slope, where he found his brigade commander, Colonel I. B. Richardson, together with the rest of the brigade and General Tyler. Tyler had just ordered two guns to a forward position when Captain J. B. Fry, the chief of McDowell's staff, appeared. Fry asked Tyler to cease fighting. But Tyler's blood was up by this time. He sent the guns forward and, when they were forced back by enemy fire, he ordered Colonel Richardson to lead two of his regiments into the attack. Richardson's nickname was 'Fighting Dick'. He was never one to hold back if a fight was in prospect, and now he led the 12th New York Regiment down the hill, with the 1st Massachusetts in support.

The Southern forces had used the interval to bring up reinforcements – Longstreet's reserve

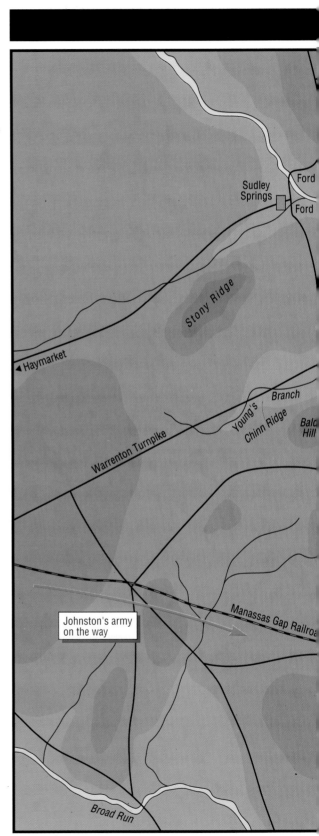

The Affair at Blackburn's Ford, 18 July

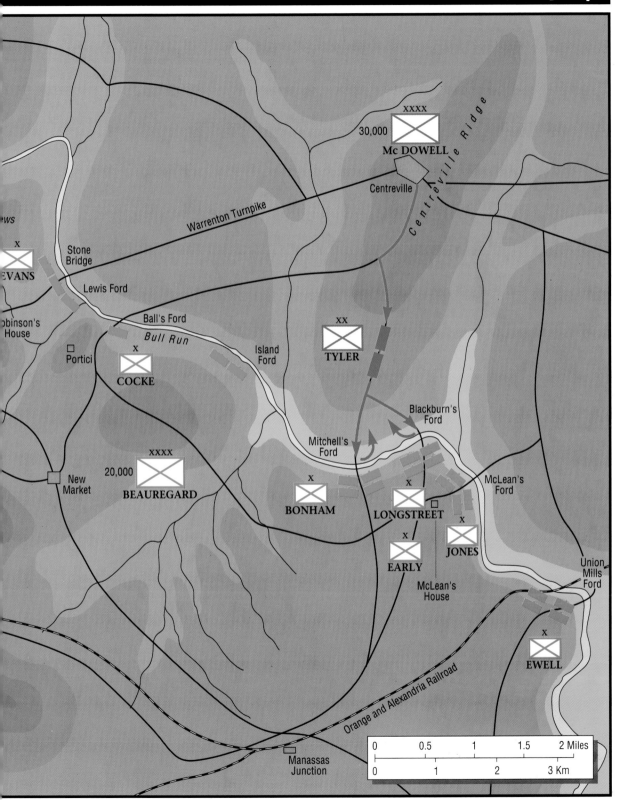

companies and men from Colonel Jubal Early's Sixth Brigade. So when the 12th New York emerged on the open ground above the river, and within range of the enemy's muskets, they came under fiercer fire than their predecessors had suffered. They took cover, returned fire and endured for half an hour. Then they ran.

When they saw this, Longstreet's men crossed the ford and launched themselves at the 1st Massachusetts Regiment, now cruelly exposed, and they too were forced to retreat back up the hill.

Richardson wanted to mount another attack. He had three regiments that had not yet been involved, and Sherman was bringing up his brigade at the double. Together, Richardson argued, they could 'clear out those fellows from the bottom in two hours'. But Tyler now felt he had gone far enough. He ordered a re-grouping behind the crest of the hill to repulse any Southern attack. No attack came.

Tyler Rebuked

Shortly before 4 p.m. McDowell rode up to make it forcefully clear to Tyler that he had exceeded his orders, and to insist that he had no intention of fighting the main battle that day.

For a while longer the guns on both sides continued firing. By chance a stray Northern shell landed in the fireplace of the McLean House, where Beauregard had set up his headquarters and where he and his staff were about to sit down to dinner. No one was hurt, but their dinner was ruined. Beauregard promptly ordered more guns to the front to exact revenge.

Altogether, the Northern army lost 83 men in this action: 19 killed, 38 wounded and 26 missing; the South lost 70: 15 killed, 53 wounded and two missing.

Beauregard had good reason to be pleased with the day's events. The Northern attack had come in the region where he had expected it. On the whole, his men had stood up well to their initiation. It had been a minor engagement, but such honours as there were certainly belonged to the South. His army's morale was strengthened. The auguries seemed good. But Beauregard was afraid that the main attack would be launched next morning,

before Jo Johnston had time to bring his army to the field. The affair at Blackburn's Ford took place in the afternoon of Thursday 18 July. This was the day when Johnston started to move his army from Winchester to Manassas. They would not start to arrive until the next afternoon. In Beauregard's view, they would be too late. 'McDowell will be upon us early tomorrow', he told his staff, 'when we must fight him and sell our lives as dearly as possible.'

But McDowell, too, had much on his mind. The day had not gone well for him. General Tyler had shown a dangerous independence of spirit. Some of the volunteer soldiers had retreated in disorder. In an article he wrote later, Captain Fry, McDowell's assistant adjutant general, said: 'The Confederates, feeling that they had repulsed a heavy and real attack, were encouraged by the result. The Federal troops, on the other hand, were greatly depressed. The regiment which suffered most was completely demoralized, and McDowell thought that the depression of the repulse was felt throughout the army.'

Worst of all for McDowell was the fact that the nature of the terrain had ruled out the flanking movement he planned from the East. He now had to find an alternative, and that would take time.

THE BATTLE PLANS

The strategic advantages lay with Beauregard. His men were defending what they now regarded as their own separate homeland from the aggressor. He was operating on interior lines, well-served by railways. He had had time to survey the terrain and to prepare his defences in country that provided plenty of cover. Because the soldiers and many of the officers on both sides were largely untrained, it made best sense to hold his men in position and let the enemy charge at them, uphill, wasting strength.

But such a scheme did not accord with Beauregard's grandiloquent notions of military splendour. Time and again, in the days before the battle, he came up with impractical and potentially disastrous ideas. On 13 July he wrote to Johnston urging him to leave a token force in the Shenandoah Valley and bring the bulk of his army to Manassas, whence the two of them would advance to destroy first McDowell, then Patterson, then General McClellan's smaller army in West Virginia. Within a month, he claimed, at one brilliant stroke, the war would be won. He sent one of his staff, Colonel James Chesnut, to Richmond to present the plan to President Davis and General Lee. The listened politely, expressed admiration, then pointed out that Beauregard's assessment of his army's strength was greatly exaggerated, his assessment of its capabilities hopelessly optimistic.

A few days later, when McDowell's army started its march, Beauregard devised another aggressive scheme. He felt sure the Northerners would attack at Mitchell's Ford. As soon as this attack began, Longstreet and other brigades farther downstream would cross the river and hurl themselves at the enemy's left flank and rear, threatening Centreville. It was another wild plan. It depended on the enemy doing exactly what Beauregard expected him to do, made no provision for anything else, and exaggerated the capabilities of his own units. Fortunately, there was no prospect of its being attempted.

After the affair at Blackburn's Ford, when Johnston was at Piedmont station arranging his army's transport to Manassas, Beauregard proposed an even more unworkable scheme. Johnston should split his force in two. Half of them would go to Manassas and link up with Beauregard's army. The other half would march north of the railway, traverse the Bull Run Mountains and fall upon McDowell's right flank. Johnston later commented: 'I did not agree to the plan because, ordinarily, it is impracticable to direct the movements of troops so distant from each other, by roads so far separated, in such a manner as to combine their action on a field of battle.' At the time, he did not respond to Beauregard's suggestion. He merely sent a message to say his whole army was making for Manassas Junction.

The first of Jackson's Virginians reached Piedmont at 6 a.m. on Friday 19 July. The loading took a long time and, since there was only one locomotive available, it travelled very carefully. It was not until late that afternoon that they reached Manassas Junction. The train then hurried back for its next load, two regiments of Colonel Barstow's Brigade, men from Georgia and Kentucky. It was 8 a.m. on Saturday when they arrived at Manasass. The shuttle service speeded up when another train was commandeered. Johnston travelled with General Bee's Brigade (from Alabama and Mississippi and Tennessee) to reach Beauregard's headquarters about midday.

◀ *Colonel Israel B. Richardson, known as 'Fighting Dick', commanded the 4th Brigade of Tyler's Division, men from New York and Massachusetts. They were in action on 18 July but* *had little to do on the day of the main battle. (Anne S. K. Brown Mil. Coll., BUL)*

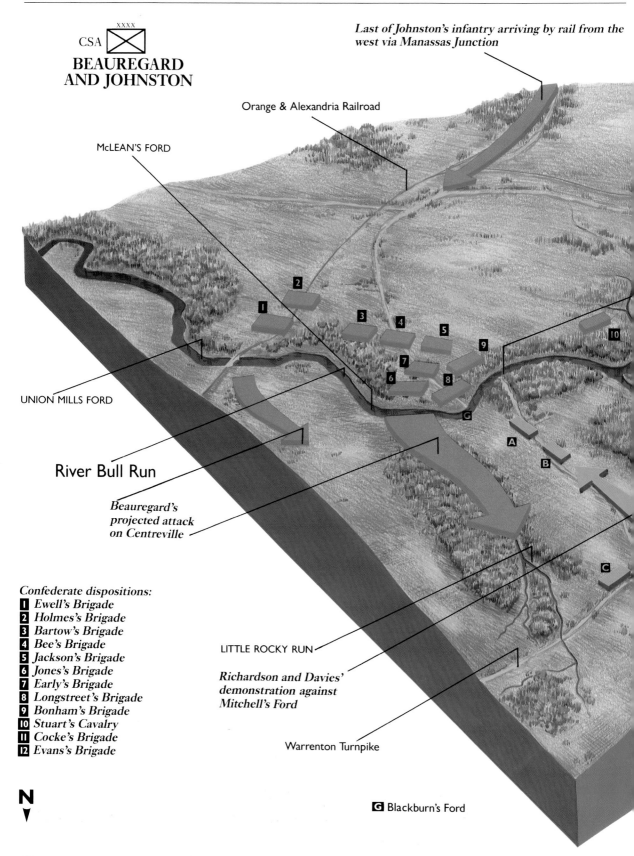

CSA

**BEAUREGARD
AND JOHNSTON**

Last of Johnston's infantry arriving by rail from the west via Manassas Junction

Orange & Alexandria Railroad

McLEAN'S FORD

UNION MILLS FORD

River Bull Run

*Beauregard's
projected attack
on Centreville*

Confederate dispositions:
1 *Ewell's Brigade*
2 *Holmes's Brigade*
3 *Bartow's Brigade*
4 *Bee's Brigade*
5 *Jackson's Brigade*
6 *Jones's Brigade*
7 *Early's Brigade*
8 *Longstreet's Brigade*
9 *Bonham's Brigade*
10 *Stuart's Cavalry*
11 *Cocke's Brigade*
12 *Evans's Brigade*

LITTLE ROCKY RUN

*Richardson and Davies'
demonstration against
Mitchell's Ford*

Warrenton Turnpike

N
▼

G Blackburn's Ford

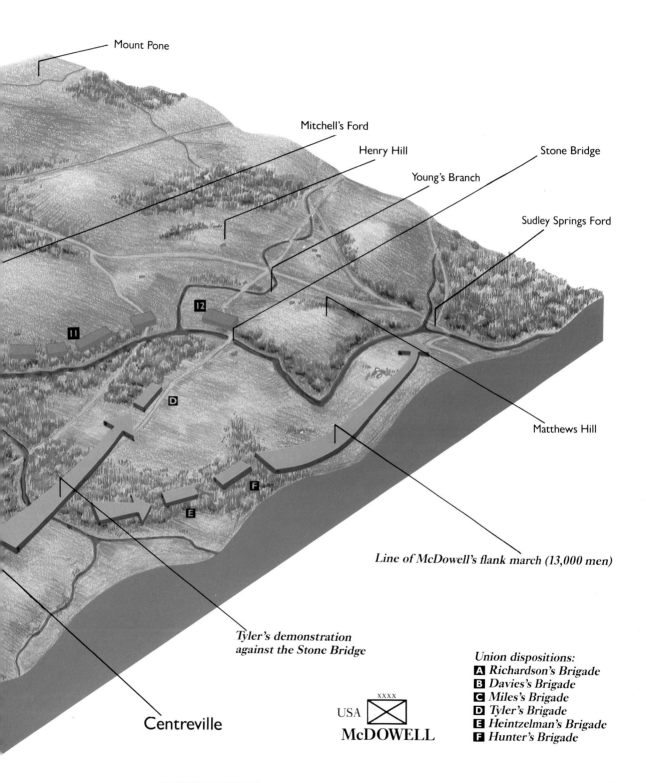

Mount Pone

Mitchell's Ford

Henry Hill

Young's Branch

Stone Bridge

Sudley Springs Ford

Matthews Hill

12

11

D

F

E

Line of McDowell's flank march (13,000 men)

Tyler's demonstration
against the Stone Bridge

Centreville

USA ⊠ McDOWELL

Union dispositions:
A *Richardson's Brigade*
B *Davies's Brigade*
C *Miles's Brigade*
D *Tyler's Brigade*
E *Heintzelman's Brigade*
F *Hunter's Brigade*

POSITIONS AND PLANS

on the eve of battle; as seen from the north.

Beauregard was a relieved man. No mention seems to have been made of his idea that Johnston should split his force in two. Half of it had now reached the Bull Run front and the rest was on the way. Further reinforcements were coming by rail from Richmond. And for two vital days, 19 and 20 July, McDowell had made no move.

There were two things McDowell had to do on the 19th. His men had run out of food, so fresh supplies had to be brought up in order that each man might go into battle with two days' rations in his haversack. The other task was to find a way, to the west, by which he might out-flank the enemy line. There was known to be a good ford, wide enough for wheeled vehicles, across the river at a place called Sudley Springs. He needed to be sure that the road to the ford would permit the reasonably trouble-free passage of two divisions, some 13,000 men.

He sent an engineering officer with a cavalry escort to find out. They rode a few miles along the road but had to turn back before reaching the ford because they ran into enemy patrols and did not want to arouse suspicion. It seemed a reasonable assumption that this was a feasible way to Sudley Springs, but McDowell wanted to be absolutely sure. So further patrols were sent, and it was not until midday on Saturday 20th that his engineers could assure him the route was practicable. In effect, a second day had been wasted.

McDowell knew he could delay no longer. Already some of his three-month' volunteers, the 4th Pennsylvania Regiment and the gunners of the 8th New York, were packing up to go, rejecting all pleas to stay for the fight. That night McDowell told his commanders his plans for the battle.

McDowell's Plan

The affair at Blackburn's Ford had convinced McDowell that it was in this area that the enemy expected his main attack. It was here, he felt sure, that Beauregard had concentrated his defences. McDowell was right. With this in mind, then, he decided to feint an attack here but send his main striking force round to the west to fall on the enemy's left flank and rear, severing the railway line before Johnston could reach the field – there were rumours that Johnston was already on the way, but McDowell dismissed them.

On the evening of Saturday 20 July, McDowell issued his orders. Tyler's First Division would stage the feint attack on the Stone Bridge, 'making proper demonstrations'. Richardson's brigade would make similar threatening gestures towards Blackburn's Ford. The Fifth Division, commanded by Colonel D. S. Miles, would stay in reserve behind them, in the Centreville area. Meanwhile the Second and Third Divisions, totalling more than 13,000 men, would march westwards in the dark, cross the river at Sudley Springs at dawn, out-flank the enemy and carry the day. McDowell himself would be with them.

It was a simple and reasonable plan. Perhaps it would have been wiser to launch his feint attacks farther downstream, more distant from the flanking movement. There was also the danger, if Johnston's army was arriving, that the flanking force would come up against Southern soldiers comparatively fresh from their train journey. But the biggest flaw in McDowell's plan lay in the detail of its timing. His first intention was that his columns should move off that evening and cover some miles before bivouacking. But several of his commanders argued that the men should be allowed to rest until the early hours of Sunday morning, and McDowell allowed himself to be persuaded. It was a mistake on two counts: the night march proved something of a nightmare; and McDowell was able to consume one of his colossal suppers, with the result that he felt seriously unwell next morning.

Southern Plans

On the farther side of the river, too, plans were being made and given for the morrow's battle. The first problem, when Johnston arrived at Beauregard's headquarters, was to determine who was in overall command. Johnston was not in any doubt about this. He out-ranked Beauregard and had taken the precaution, a few day's before, of getting confirmation from President Davis that he was to be in charge. Even so, in his account of the battle that was published after the Civil War, Beauregard gave a very different impression: 'General Johnston was the ranking officer, and entitled, there-fore, to assume command of the united forces; but as the extensive field of operations was one which I had occupied since the beginning of June, and with which I was thoroughly familiar in all its extent and military bearings, while he was wholly unacquainted with it, and, moreover, as I had made my plans and dispositions for the maintenance of the position, General Johnston, in view of the gravity of the impending issue, preferred not to assume the responsibilities of the chief direction of the forces during the battle, but to assist me upon the field. Thereupon, I explained my plans and purposes, to which he agreed.' It is characteristic Beauregard. He lacked most of his hero, Napoleon's, skills as a commander but had all his assiduity in the favourable rewriting of history.

It was Johnston who took command. But he was a tired man by the time he reached Manassas and wise enough to recognize that Beauregard knew the terrain and the current dispositions far better than he did. So he listened while Beauregard expounded the situation and his plans, gave his approval and went off to catch up on some sleep. Both generals agreed that the battle would have to take place next day. Otherwise, there was a danger that Patterson might arrive to tilt the balance of strength heavily against them.

Beauregard and his staff settled down to write out the orders. His plan was, of course, an aggressive one. His line extended some six miles, from Union Bridge on the right, the point where the railway crossed the river, to Stone Bridge on the left, where the river was spanned by the Warrenton Turnpike road. Despite the setback the Northern army had suffered two days earlier at Blackburn's Ford, Beauregard still clung to his conviction that the main enemy thrust would come in that region, at Mitchell's Ford especially. So he had placed the bulk of his army, two-thirds of his men, on the right and right-centre of his line, with Johnston's men behind them in support. His left flank, where the river offered the best crossing points, he planned to guard with a brigade and a half, just over 4,000 men. At daybreak on Sunday morning, Beauregard ordered, his leading brigades in the centre would force their way across the river and, supported by the others, drive a way uphill towards Centreville in the area where he expected to find the bulk of McDowell's army.

It was a rash and ill-considered plan and the orders to his commanders were ill-written, unclear and sometimes downright impenetrable. It was a matter of the greatest good fortune for the Southern cause that it proved impossible even to begin to try and implement the plan.

That Saturday night was calm and lovely. On both sides of the river thousands of men lay on the ground, gazing at the starry sky and wondering what the next day would bring. The great majority of them, who had never been in action, tried to imagine what it would be like and worried about how they would behave under fire, whether they would disgrace themselves under the eyes of their comrades and old friends, whether they would see another night sky. All the big talk in the bars, all the parades and speeches and cheering girls were behind them now, and tomorrow they would come face to face with the reality. Even those officers who had known battle before had experienced nothing as big as this.

On the Northern side there had been many visitors to the camps during the day. The pioneer photograper, Mathew Brady, was there with his bulky equipment: 'We are making history now,' he said, 'and every picture that we get will be valuable.' There were many newspaper reporters in the camps. The editor of the *New York Times*, Henry J. Raymond, wrote to his paper: 'This is one of the most beautiful nights that the imagination can conceive. The sky is perfectly clear, the moon is full and bright, and the air as still as if it were not within a few hours to be disturbed by the roar of canon and the shouts of contending men . . . An hour ago I rode back to General McDowell's headquarters . . . As I rose over the crest of the hill, and caught a view of the scene in front, it seemed a picture of enchantment. The bright moon cast the woods which bound the field into deep shadows, through which the camp fires shed a clear and brilliant glow. On the extreme right, in the neighbourhood of the Fire Zouaves, a party were singing "The Star-spangled Banner", and from the left rose the sweet strains of a magnificent band, intermingling opera airs with patriotic bursts of "Hail Columbia" and "Yankee Doodle" . . .

Dawn 21 July: positions of opposing forces before Tyler's gun

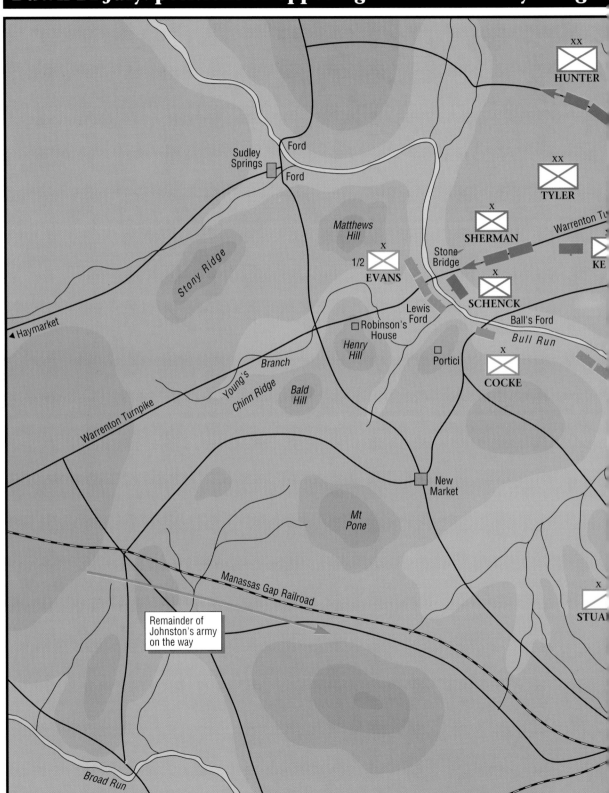

HUNTER

Ford

Sudley
Springs

Ford

TYLER

Matthews
Hill

SHERMAN

Warrenton T

EVANS

Stone
Bridge

KE

Stony Ridge

SCHENCK

Lewis
Ford

Ball's Ford

Haymarket

Robinson's
House

Portici

Bull Run

Henry
Hill

COCKE

Branch

Young's
Chinn Ridge

Bald
Hill

Warrenton Turnpike

New
Market

Mt
Pone

Manassas Gap Railroad

STUAR

Remainder of
Johnston's army
on the way

Broad Run

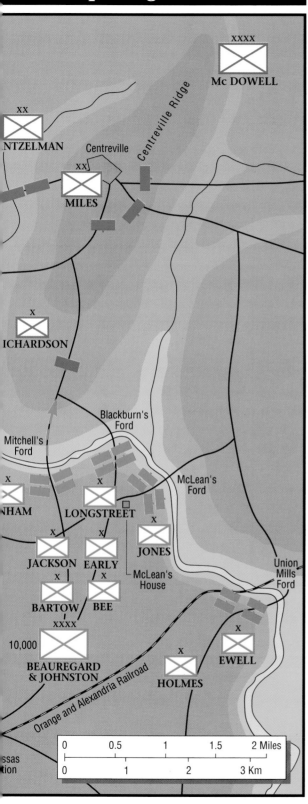

THE BATTLE BEGINS

Reveille was sounded in Tyler's Division at 2 a.m. on Sunday 21 July. The idea was that Tyler's three brigades – Schenck's, then Sherman's, then Keyes' – would move off smartly and leave the road clear for the two divisions that had the long flanking march to make.

It did not work out like that. Men had trouble getting their gear together in the dark; the officers had trouble getting their men together. Schenck placed skirmishers on either side of the road, volunteer soldiers from Ohio, and they had a terrible time hacking their way through tangled undergrowth. Meanwhile his artillerymen and their horses were struggling to move their enormous 30-pounder canon, weighing three tons, along the road. The first half mile took them an hour. For the men marching behind, it meant endless stops and starts, long periods of standing and wondering what was going on ahead, much confusion and bad temper.

As a result, it was not until long after first light, sometime after 6 a.m., that the 30-pounder gun fired three rounds across the Bull Run as a signal to McDowell that Tyler was in position at last to begin his 'proper demonstrations' at the Stone Bridge. It was also a signal to all the men of both armies that the battle was about to start.

The shells flew high over the heads of the small brigade that Beauregard had posted at the Stone Bridge on the extreme left of his line. The whole force was no more than 1,100 men – the 4th South Carolina Regiment and the 1st Louisiana, with two canon and a handful of cavalry. Their commander, though, was a formidable figure, Colonel Nathan G. Evans. Evans was a young man, 37 years old and full of fire. He came from South Carolina, graduated from West Point in 1848 and took part in a few minor Indian campaigns. He was a character, careless of reputation or rank, wild in manner, a great drinker and

51

▲Colonel Nathan G. ('Shanks') Evans was a fiery and uncouth officer, but his independent initiative on the morning of Bull Run and the skill of his fighting proved invaluable to the Southern cause. He held Tyler at the Stone Bridge, then – when he saw his army's left flank under serious threat – moved the bulk of his small brigade to Matthews Hill, where he fought another ferocious and successful defensive action. He later claimed that he 'and a few private gentlemen' had won the battle – with some help from the Almighty.

curser and bragger. An orderly was deputed to keep close at hand, with a one-gallon drum of whisky on his back to keep the colonel well-fuelled. His nick-name was 'Shanks'. He loved a rough-house and felt unfairly starved, so far, of action. This Sunday morning was to put that right. But there was more to 'Shanks' Evans than just a bar-room brawler: he had a sharp eye for the way a battle was developing and the confidence to take important decisions promptly, on his own initiative. This acute, pugnacious personality was to have a major influence on the course of events at Bull Run. For the moment, though, as Tyler's guns thundered and his men moved gingerly down the slope towards the Stone Bridge, Evans held his

fire, giving the enemy no indication of his strength or of his positions.

The Flank March

The roar of the big gun was heard by the divisional commanders of the flanking march, Colonel Hunter and Colonel Heintzelman, with dismay. They were some three hours behind their schedule. They were already late when they turned right off the Warrenton Turnpike and struck across country. The road they had been told to follow was a cart track, mostly through woods. The men who led, the 2nd Rhode Island Regiment of Colonel Burnside's brigade, had to use axes and picks and shovels to clear the way and widen the track. It was already warm, promising a day of intense summer heat. To make matters worse, their guide chose a wrong turning that added some three miles to their march. It was almost 9 o'clock when they emerged from the trees and began the gentle descent across open fields to the ford at Sudley Springs.

McDowell was with this column. At first he had felt so unwell he had travelled in a carriage; then he switched to horseback to move up and down the line urging his men forward. By going with the flank march he effectively relinquished control of the overall battle, but his other commanders had clear orders and he opted to go where he believed – rightly in the event – the vital action would take place.

The Southern commanders, too, in a different way, were already beginning to lose control over the course of events. McDowell's early start pre-empted Beauregard's aggressive plans. Beauregard and Johnston continued to hope that it might become possible, at some stage, to mount the attack with which they could threaten Centreville, but for the moment they had to wait and see what McDowell was up to. Their command system was already breaking down. Beauregard sometimes forgot to pass vital information on to his brigade commanders, and many of his messages never reached their destinations. Those that did arrive were often ambiguous and confusing. When Beauregard saw Tyler's brigades on the high ground beyond the Stone Bridge, he realized that

Evans' tiny force could not be expected to hold them at bay for long. So he ordered the brigades of Jackson, Bee and Bartow to move quickly to positions behind Evans.

On the far side of the river, General Tyler was acting with extreme caution. He had deployed Sherman's brigade on the northern side of the Turnpike, Schenck's on the South. According to Sherman's official report, they then 'remained quietly in position till after 10 a.m.'. Activity was confined to the firing of their artillery and a little tentative skirmishing towards the bridge.

Only three days before, Tyler had been admonished for exceeding his orders at Black-

burn's Ford. Now he went to the opposite extreme. There seems little doubt that had he made vigorous efforts to take the bridge while it was still feebly defended – he outnumbered Evan's brigade by more than seven-to-one – he could have established a firm foothold on the far bank of the river and distracted the enemy's attention from the flank march. But he stuck to the letter of his orders and did little.

By 8 o'clock that morning Evans felt sure the enemy's move towards the Stone Bridge was a feint. Half an hour later he saw clouds of dust two miles away to the north and guessed that a big enemy column was moving round to attack from the west. Shortly afterwards the flank march was spotted by Beauregard's Chief Signal Officer, Captain Alexander. Edward Porter Alexander was an intelligent and conscientious officer. He had been the star pupil of the pioneer of visual signalling in the field, Dr. Albert J. Myer, an army surgeon who had devised a method of sending messages considerable distances by flag signals ('wigwagging') in daytime, by torches at night.

▼ *The Stone Bridge carries the Warrenton Turnpike across River Bull Run. It played a vital part in the battle. At the start of the day it marked the extreme left of the Southern defensive line and was guarded by Colonel 'Shanks' Evans's small brigade. Unfortunately for the Northern cause, Tyler's attack was so feebly maintained that Evans was able to hold the bridge and move farther left to delay the advance of McDowell's flank movement.*

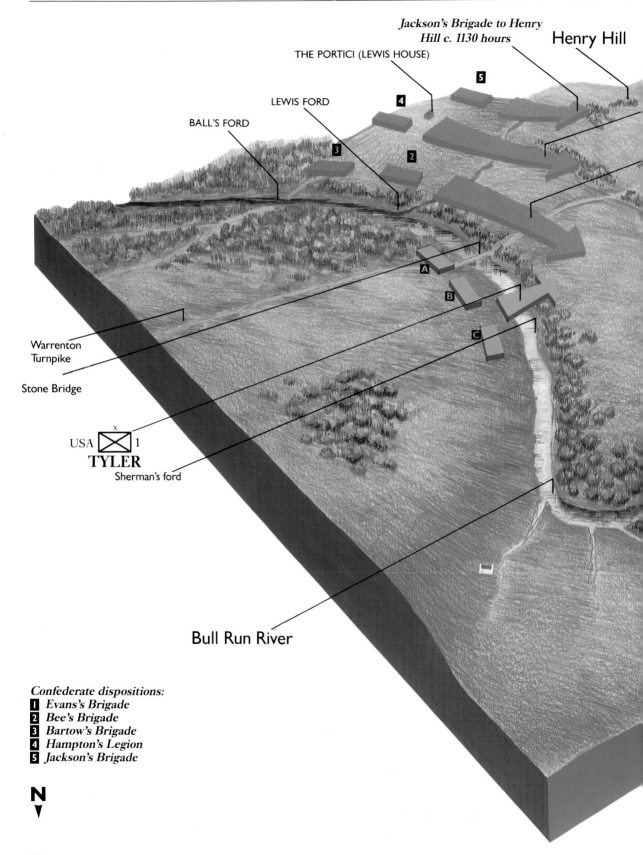

Jackson's Brigade to Henry Hill c. 1130 hours

Henry Hill

THE PORTICI (LEWIS HOUSE)

5

LEWIS FORD

4

BALL'S FORD

3

2

A

B

C

Warrenton
Turnpike

Stone Bridge

USA ⊠ 1
TYLER
Sherman's ford

Bull Run River

Confederate dispositions:
1 *Evans's Brigade*
2 *Bee's Brigade*
3 *Bartow's Brigade*
4 *Hampton's Legion*
5 *Jackson's Brigade*

N
▼

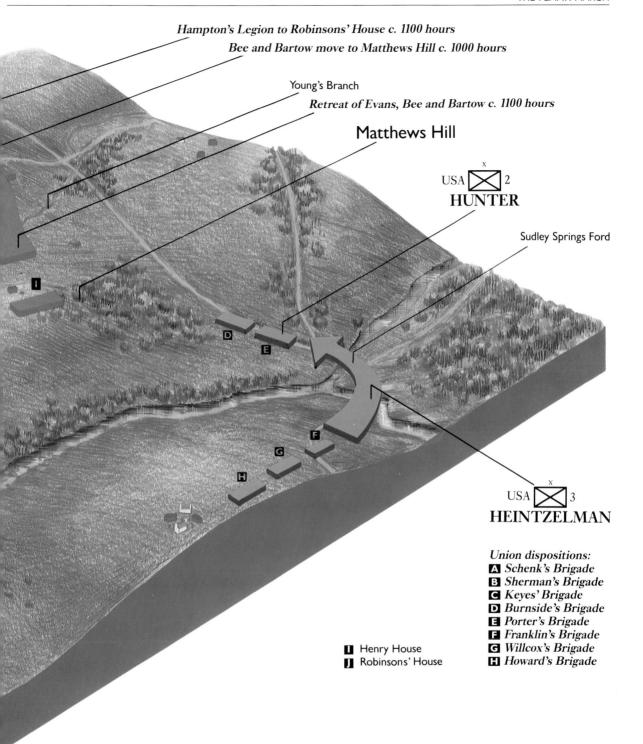

Hampton's Legion to Robinsons' House c. 1100 hours

Bee and Bartow move to Matthews Hill c. 1000 hours

Young's Branch

Retreat of Evans, Bee and Bartow c. 1100 hours

Matthews Hill

USA ⊠ 2
HUNTER

Sudley Springs Ford

USA ⊠ 3
HEINTZELMAN

Union dispositions:
A *Schenk's Brigade*
B *Sherman's Brigade*
C *Keyes' Brigade*
D *Burnside's Brigade*
E *Porter's Brigade*
F *Franklin's Brigade*
G *Willcox's Brigade*
H *Howard's Brigade*

I Henry House
J Robinsons' House

MATTHEWS HILL

as seen from the north. The situation at 0915 hours (and subsequently) when Evans's firing on Hunter's leading brigade announced the beginning of the main battle.

▲ Colonel Ambrose E. Burnside is oddly immortalised in the English language by the word that now designates his style in whiskers – 'sideburns'. It was his brigade that was first halted by 'Shanks' Evans in position on Matthews Hill. From then on, they were in the thick of the action until the retreat in the late afternoon. (Anne S. K. Brown Mil. Coll., BUL)

▲ David Hunter commanded the 2nd Division of the Northern army, which led the big flanking movement. 21 July marked his 59th birthday: he celebrated by getting wounded in the initial engagement at Matthews Hill and had to hand over his command to Burnside. (Anne S. K. Brown Mil. Coll., BUL)

Alexander was a young man – he had graduated from West Point only four years before – and ambitious. For weeks before the battle he had been busy setting up lookout and signal platforms and training his men in the codes. He had been rudely awakened that morning when the second shell from Tyler's 30-pounder tore through the roof of his tent. Now, shortly before 9 a.m., he was surveying the scene by telescope from his headquarters signal tower when he saw the morning sunlight glinting on canon and bayonets far away to the north. Immediately he signalled to Evans: 'Look out for your left. You are turned.'

Evans Moves

It confirmed what Evans already suspected, and he acted immediately. Leaving only four companies to cover the bridge, he took the rest of his men and two six-pounder guns as rapidly as possible to his left and found an excellent position on Matthews Hill. There was good tree cover for his riflemen and his guns as well as a fine view across the open ground the Northerners would have to cross. He placed the 4th South Carolina Regiment on the left with one gun; the 1st Louisiana on the right with the other. Soon after that, the 4th Alabama Regiment arrived to help. They were just in time.

It was about 9.15 when the leading column of McDowell's flanking force, men of the 1st Rhode Island Regiment, emerged from the woods below Matthews Hill. Evans immediately fired a volley. The real battle had begun.

The commander of the Second Brigade of the Second Division, which now came under fire, was a most imposing military figure, Colonel Ambrose E. Burnside. He sported a magnificent black moustache and luxuriant side-whiskers so impressive that he gave a new word to the English language – 'sideburns'. He was a West Point graduate who had seen action against the Apaches, but that was years ago. He retired from the army in 1853 to go into business, manufacturing a breech-loading rifle. When the Civil War broke out he re-enlisted, raised the 1st Rhode Island Regiment, took command as its colonel and soon afterwards was in charge of a brigade. There were two Rhode Island regiments in the brigade and the young governor of Rhode Island, William Sprague, although a civilian had come along too, to see how the boys acquitted themselves.

Evans' initial volley took them by surprise. They were not expecting to meet the enemy so soon. And they were tired. The day was already hot and they had been on their feet, stopping and marching and clearing a way, for more than six hours. It was with difficulty that Burnside got his riflemen spread out into line. They began to return the enemy's fire, though he was not easy to see.

The divisional commander, Brigadier General David Hunter, was on the scene very quickly. He had served nearly 40 years in the army but had never been in action. It was his 59th birthday, and he was to see more than enough action in the next few minutes. He struggled to get the rest of Burnside's brigade into battle line and the batteries into position to answer the fire of Evan's guns, then led infantry and artillery towards the enemy, up the gentle lower slopes of the hill. They came under intense fire, and Hunter was badly wounded in his left cheek and neck. As he was being carried from the field, he told Burnside, 'I leave the matter in your hands.'

The general standard of infantry marksmanship at Bull Run was poor. Most of the raw recruits made the mistake of firing too high. But the fire that Colonel Evans brought to bear was unusually effective. Colonel John Slocum of the Second Rhode Island was mortally wounded in this fierce little action. Burnside had his horse shot from under him. The Northern forces, superior in numbers to Evans's from the start and increasing in strength all the time as fresh columns arrived, were effectively halted. For the second time that day 'Shanks' Evans proved he had the knack of giving the enemy the impression that his forces were far stronger than they were – Burnside thought he was dealing with at least six infantry regiments and two, probably more, full batteries of artillery.

But Evans knew he could not hold out indefinitely against the force that was building up against him. He had two guns and about 900 men, holding off Hunter's two brigades, a total of nearly 6,000 men and several batteries. On top of that, Heintzelman's brigades were rapidly approaching. Evans played for time cleverly. Sending urgent messages requesting reinforcement, he launched the men of the 1st Louisiana Regiment, known as 'Wheat's Tigers', in an attack on the re-forming Northern line. Major Roberdeau Wheat, a very tough individual, led the charge and was severely wounded. They were beaten back but not before they had further hardened the Northerners' belief that they were dealing with a considerable and confident body of men.

Reinforcements Arrive

Evans was vastly relieved when he saw support arriving: General Barnard E. Bee with two-and-a-half regiments, closely followed by Colonel Francis Bartow with two regiments of Georgians. The arrival, at the double, of some 2,800 men did much to redress the imbalance. It was shortly after 10 a.m..

Evans had stalled the Northerners' advance for almost an hour and endured much, especially from the expert gunfire of Charles Griffin and J. B. Ricketts. It was time to hand over to fresh men.

General Bee had all of Evans's relish for a good fight. He had distinguished himself in the Mexican War but had been starved of fighting since then, and his great concern on the morning of Bull Run was that he might miss the action. He was furious when he was moved to the Stone Bridge area because he was sure the real fight would be elsewhere. He waited as patiently as he could, listening to the noise of the intensifying battle a mile or more to his left, and finally determined, on his own initiative, to double towards the sound of the guns. Together with his artillery commander, Captain John D.Imboden, he galloped to the top of Henry Hill, surveyed the scene and said: 'Here is the battlefield and we are

▲*Brigadier Barnard E. Bee of South Carolina commanded the 3rd Brigade of Johnston's army, the first unit of that army to get into the fight proper. As Evans had done before him, he shifted his men to the far left of the line when he saw that that was where the action was.*

He arrived in the nick of time to save Evans, and from then on he and his men were at the heart of the fight. It was he who likened Jackson's stand to a stone wall. Soon after that, Bee, riding at the head of his brigade, was mortally wounded.

▲*Colonel Francis Bartow, commander of Johnston's 2nd Brigade, was quick to follow Bee's Brigade to the threatened left of the line, with two regiments of Georgians, He took part in the desperate charge against the Northern lines at Matthews Hill, then in the battle for Henry Hill.*

He was killed on Henry Hill. (Anne S. K. Brown Mil. Coll., BUL)

in for it! Bring up your guns as quickly as possible, and I'll look round for a good position.'

Bee marched his men (volunteers from Alabama and Mississippi) down the hill, formed them into line and established them on Evan's right. Behind him came Bartow with his Georgians, and they positioned themselves with their guns on Bee's right. Now the line of Southerners – Evans, Bee and Bartow – planned to launch themselves in a desperate attack, hoping to overrun and silence the Northern batteries that had been pounding them hard.

They charged downhill towards the brigades of Burnside and Porter who, as the senior, was now in command. One of Bartow's Georgians said two days later: 'This bold and fearful movement was made through a perfect storm.' When they had fired a volley, the Northern line rose and advanced. Within moments the battle dissolved into a confused, short-range turmoil. 'It was a whirlwind

of bullets,' one man remembered. Many men fell, killed or wounded. The toll was heaviest among the officers. Units found themselves leaderless and lost. In the end, as it had to do, the sheer weight of the Northern numbers turned the scales, and the Southerners retreated back up the hill in disarray.

McDowell was anxious. The stubborn resistance of the Southerners had now held up his outflanking movement by nearly two hours, and clouds of dust in the distance towards Manassas meant the enemy had more units on the way. But he too could summon up reinforcements. He sent orders to Tyler, still virtually becalmed above the Stone Bridge, to press his attacks much more vigorously. And at last (it was now about 11 a.m.) the leading brigades of Heintzelman's Division – men from Massachusetts and Minnesota – were moving up to the front.

Heintzelman was 56. He had fought with distinction against the Mexicans and the Indians, but he was a prickly, short-tempered man, and the morning so far had been a succession of frustrations. He arrived on the scene just as the Southern regiments were pulling back up Matthews Hill. At first the Northern line was in almost as much confusion as that of the retreating Southerners. Heintzelman could find no one who seemed to be in command. Then McDowell appeared and immediately ordered Heintzelman to use his fresh regiments to keep up the pressure on the enemy. He tried a frontal attack, but it was beaten back. He sent two regiments – the 11th New York and Ellsworth's Zouaves – round to the right to attack the enemy flank, but they were held off by Evans, who had managed to re-group his diminishing force. Heintzelman was planning a third assault when he saw the enemy pulling back from the top of Matthews Hill. Bartow had seen

another powerful enemy force approaching from the north – this was Sherman's brigade, 3,400 strong.

Sherman Joins In

After the initial march down the Warrenton Turnpike in the early hours, Sherman's men had had a quiet time. Sherman used it to reconnoitre along the river bank, upstream from the Stone Bridge, to see if there was a possible crossing place. He was in luck. As he watched, a Southern horseman rode down the slope on the opposite side of the river, disappeared briefly, then re-appeared on the near side to shout some words of taunting abuse. Sherman did not react. He had found out what he wanted. Close at hand, here was a fording place not so exposed to the enemy as the

▲ Brigadier General S. P. Heintzelman commanded the 3rd Division of the Federal army, which marched behind Hunter's Division on the flank march by way of Sudley Springs. As a result, his

brigades were into action later than Hunter's, but they were very heavily involved in the fight for control of Henry Hill. (Anne S. K. Brown Mil. Coll., BUL)

▲ The point on the River Bull Run, slightly upstream of the Stone Bridge, where Sherman's sharp eyes had noticed a Southern horseman fording the stream earlier in the morning. He got his

brigade across here without difficulty when the order came to join the battle on Matthews Hill.

Stone Bridge itself and which did not involve the long detour to Sudley Springs. When the order came, shortly after 11 a.m., to join the battle on Matthews Hill, he took his brigade – with the 69th New York in the lead – comfortably across the ford, though he had to leave his artillery behind.

Sherman's initial worry was about the problem of identification. Some of his regiments were in grey uniforms, and he was afraid they would be fired upon by their own side as they advanced. In the event, the first sizeable force they came upon were the enemy, General Bee's 4th Alabama Regiment. The Alabamans were deceived and held their fire. The volley from the 69th New York killed the colonel of the 4th Alabama and seriously wounded the major, leaving them leaderless. They retreated hastily.

The retreat was very close to being a rout, but Sherman did not pursue the enemy as he fell back across the Warrenton Turnpike and up the slopes of Henry Hill beyond. It was necessary first to find his fellow commanders and work to a concerted plan. He deployed his brigade behind that of Colonel Porter, who told him Hunter had been wounded and that McDowell was in the area. He found McDowell, who was feeling much better than he had been earlier that morning.

Victory, McDowell felt, was now within his grasp. The enemy was on the run. The arrival of Sherman, with Keyes' Brigade close behind him, meant that he had succeeded in concentrating more than half his army on the weak and now sorely battered left flank of the enemy line. One more push, it seemed, and the day was won. Sherman's regiments were moved in line to take the centre position, with Burnside on his right and Porter on his left. The advance was sounded and, as the men moved forward, McDowell rode along the line shouting, 'Victory! Victory! The day is ours.'

▲An artist's impression of the battle, entitled 'Gen. Burnside's Brigade at the Battle of Bull Run'. Presumably, it is an effort to recapture the moment when Burnside, together with Porter's Brigade, had driven Evans, Bee and Bartow from Matthews Hill, and was preparing to attack Henry Hill. (Anne S. K. Brown Mil. Coll., BUL)

▶Frank Vizetelli's attempt to recreate the scene, soon after midday, as the Northern brigades were about to advance towards Henry Hill. (Illustrated London News, 31 August 1861)

THE FIGHT FOR HENRY HILL

Matthews Hill, between River Bull Run and the Warrenton Turnpike, declines southwards to a small tributary stream called Young's Branch, which presented no obstacle to advancing soldiers. Beyond the stream the ground rises gently, mostly through woodland, to the Warrenton Turnpike that crossed the Northern line of advance from East to West. Beyond the turnpike rise the steeper slopes of Henry Hill, dotted with trees but with much open grassland as well. It is not a particularly steep incline, but it gains height steadily for some 800 yards to reach a wide, undulating plateau with woodland on its farther side. It was here that the key encounter of the First Battle of Bull Run was to take place, a long and fierce and fluctuating struggle.

In July 1861 there were two modest houses on this hillside. A hundred yards above the turnpike, at the top of a grassy lane with split-rail fencing on each side, stood Robinson's House, the clap-board cottage of a freed slave. Almost at the top of the hill, just where it begins to level out to the summit plateau, there was a slightly grander place called Henry House. This had been the farm and family home of the man who gave his name to the hill, Dr. Isaac Henry, a retired naval surgeon. By 1861 he had been long dead, but his widow, Judith, a helpless invalid of 84, and two of their sons who were both semi-invalids, were still there, being looked after by a young Negress called Rosa Stokes. They were all in the house as the Northern army approached.

The advance of McDowell's line towards Henry Hill brought the sounds of battle closer to the two Southern commanders, Johnston and Beauregard. They were stationed at the centre of their line, on a small hill just south of Mitchell's Ford and nearly two miles to the south-east of Henry Hill. From Beauregard's point of view this was the proper place to be. He expected Mc-

Dowell's main attack in this area and planned to launch his own assault, towards Centreville, with the brigades on his immediate right.

Unfortunately, nothing seemed to be happening as he had expected. Soon after first light the enemy had appeared on the slopes beyond Mitchell's Ford, but since then, bewilderingly, he had made no strenuous effort to press ahead with his advance. At the same time, Beauregard's own orders for a push across Bull Run by the brigades on the right wing of his line – Longstreet's at Blackburn's Ford, Jones's at McLean's Ford and Ewell's (with Holmes's in support) at the railway crossing – were clearly not being implemented. In fact, Longstreet and Jones had moved their forward units across the river and formed them into line; then they waited for Ewell to join them on their right. He did not arrive. Beauregard's courier had never reached Brigadier General Ewell with the orders. The courier dispatched to

▲ Henry House as seen from the back of the Robinson House.

◄ The lane, with split-rail fencing either side, that leads from the Warrenton Turnpike to Robinson's House. It was here that Colonel Wade Hampton made the gallant and successful stand that further delayed the Northern advance.

▶ A private of the 1st Virginia Cavalry, the riders who distinguished themselves before and during (and long after) First Bull Run, under the command of Colonel 'Jeb' Stuart. Far right, a private of the 23rd Virginia Regiment. (Illustration by Michael Youens)

▲Brigadier General Richard S. Ewell, commanding Beauregard's 2nd Brigade, was desperately keen to get into the fight and was continually frustrated. It was intended that he should be part of the drive on Centreville, but – through administrative incompetence – Beauregard's orders never reached him. Like the Grand Old Duke of York, Ewell marched his men up and down all that hot summer's day and never got anywhere. (Anne S. K. Brown Mil. Coll., BUL)

▲Wade Hampton was outstanding even in an era of remarkable men. Some said he was the greatest landowner in the South. In the South Carolina state legislature he spoke out for secession. And when the Civil War came he threw everything – his fortune and his considerable energies – into raising and training his own Legion. He took 650 men to Bull Run. They only just arrived, in time, by railway from the South, but played an important part in holding up the North's attack on Henry Hill until Jackson had organized his defensive line on the summit plateau. (Anne S. K. Brown Mil. Coll., BUL)

Brigadier General Holmes also failed to deliver. Since no one on Beauregard's staff had noted the couriers' names, these failures in communication were never explained. So both generals held their positions and waited, with mounting and ill-concealed impatience. Ewell especially, 44 years old and desperately eager for action, made no secret of his feelings. Finally he got orders to advance, moved fast across the river, and then got orders to pull back again and resume a defensive position. By the end of the day, it was reckoned, Ewell's Brigade had marched and counter-marched more than twenty miles in the heat of the day without once coming to grips with the enemy. Holmes's Brigade, too, saw no action.

Johnston and Beauregard grew more and more concerned as the morning wore on and, while little was happening in front of them or to the right, a great deal was clearly going on to their left. Sometime between 11 a.m. and noon, the Signal Officer, Captain Alexander, reported that he had seen a great cloud of dust in the sky to the north-west. The two generals were afraid this marked the approach of General Patterson from the Shenandoah. At last Johnston determined to take matters into his own hands.' The battle is there,' he said to

Beauregard, pointing to the left. 'I am going.' He rode off.

Beauregard issued rapid orders. The brigades of Holmes, Early and Bonham should move, with speed, towards the sound of battle. Those of Longstreet, Jones and Ewell should resume their defensive positions south of Bull Run. Then Beauregard too galloped towards Henry Hill.

The situation on their left flank looked desperate. Evans, Bee and Bartow had been driven back from Matthews Hill in considerable disorder. For the North, reinforcements were arriving in strength. McDowell and his brigade commanders worked hard to form them into line for what they hoped would be the final big push to victory. Sherman was posted by the Sudley Springs road; what was left of Burnside's brigade was on his left; Keyes's brigade to the left of them. To the right of Sherman, Porter re-grouped his men. Two of Heintzelman's brigades, those of Colonel W. B. Franklin and Colonel O. B. Willcox, were directed to extend the right flank as they came up. It was a formidable force.

The South also had reinforcements on the way, but for the moment the only new men in the field were the 650 infantryman from South Carolina of Colonel Wade Hampton's Legion. The colonel, one of the great landowner/planters of the South, was an immensely wealthy and charismatic man. He was patriotic too for the Confederacy. The Legion was his own, raised and financed and led by him. Theirs had been an eventful day already. Shortly after first light their train from Richmond had pulled into Manassas Junction. They had made a quick breakfast and then orders came to hurry to the relief of Evans on the extreme left flank. It was a three-hour cross-country march and much had happened before they reached the summit of Henry Hill. They arrived just in time to see their own forces falling back and the enemy preparing to advance in line. Colonel Hampton led the way rapidly down the hill to the area of Robinson's House. They took position and almost immediately found themselves attacked from three sides by vastly superior numbers. They held their ground stoutly and had time to fire several volleys before they were forced to retreat back up Henry Hill. It was a purely holding operation, but a

▲ *It was shortly before noon when General Jackson arrived at the summit of Henry Hill with his 2,000 Virginians. He rapidly grasped the situation and organized his men into a superb defensive position, so good that the attacking Northern regiments were unable to break through and, in the end, wore* *themselves out in their repeated attempts. (Anne S. K. Brown Mil. Coll., BUL)*

successful one. It gave time for another new arrival to take position – General T. J. Jackson.

'Stonewall' Jackson

Jackson's Brigade – just over 2,000 Virginians with four canon – had started the day before dawn. First they were moved forward to support Longstreet; later they were ordered two miles to the left to support Bonham and Cocke. When he arrived there, Jackson heard the din of the real battle going on even farther to the left and, as Bee and Bartow had done before him, immediately pressed on. He

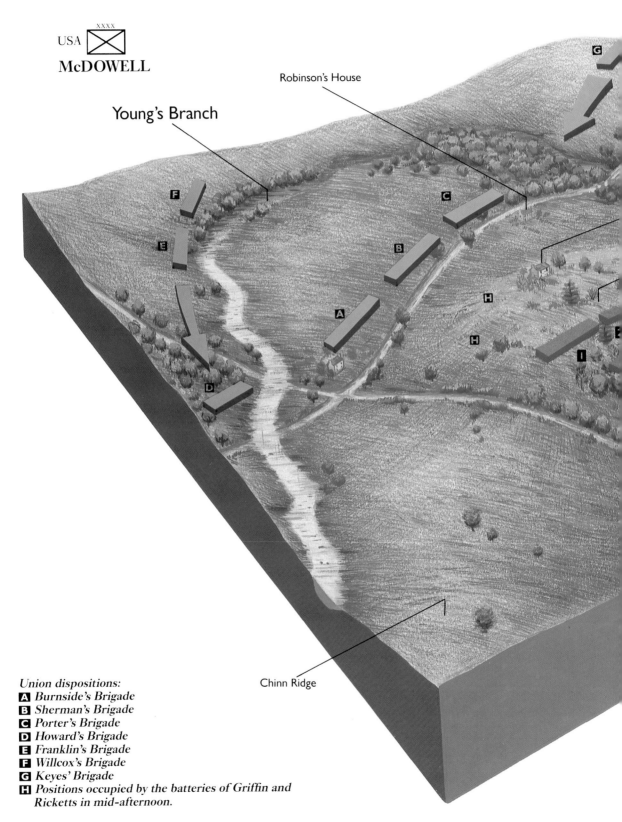

USA ⊠ ^{xxxx}
McDOWELL

Robinson's House

Young's Branch

Chinn Ridge

Union dispositions:
A *Burnside's Brigade*
B *Sherman's Brigade*
C *Porter's Brigade*
D *Howard's Brigade*
E *Franklin's Brigade*
F *Willcox's Brigade*
G *Keyes' Brigade*
H *Positions occupied by the batteries of Griffin and*
Ricketts in mid-afternoon.

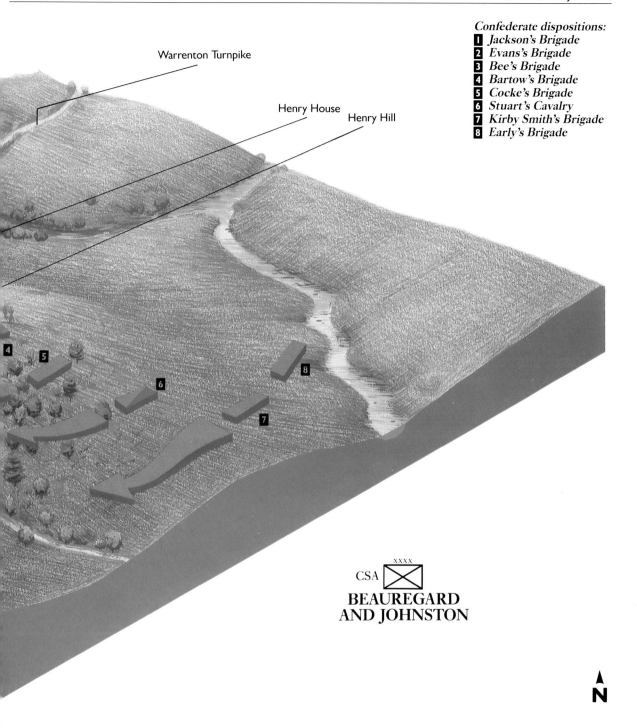

Warrenton Turnpike

Henry House

Henry Hill

Confederate dispositions:
1 *Jackson's Brigade*
2 *Evans's Brigade*
3 *Bee's Brigade*
4 *Bartow's Brigade*
5 *Cocke's Brigade*
6 *Stuart's Cavalry*
7 *Kirby Smith's Brigade*
8 *Early's Brigade*

CSA ⊠ xxxx
**BEAUREGARD
AND JOHNSTON**

N

THE FIGHT FOR HENRY HILL

**as seen from the south. Dispositions at midday, at the
commencement of the battle for Henry Hill.**

emerged from the woods on to the summit plateau of Henry Hill at about 11.30 a.m.

At that moment there was a brief lull in the fighting, both sides hurriedly re-forming their lines. Many of Bee's men – some of them wounded, others shattered by their first experience of battle – were stumbling through to the rear, speaking of defeat. As one of the Jackson's men said, it 'was not an encouraging sight to brand-new troops'.

Jackson organized his brigade into line, 150 yards or so behind the forward crest of the hill. It was an excellent position, of the type often used and recommended by the Duke of Wellington. The woods immediately behind offered good cover. The men would be invisible to the enemy guns and invisible to their infantry too until the moment when they emerged on to the plateau, within close range. In the centre of his line Jackson placed one of his own batteries and the four smooth-bore six-pounders of Captain John Imboden that had been busily pounding the enemy at the foot of the hill.

Before long they heard the battle resume. Then, to their right, they saw Bee's men in flight. To give some cover to Wade Hampton's beleaguered Legion, Jackson got his guns firing.

The infantrymen on the right of the line, lying on the grass and waiting, saw a single horseman galloping towards them. One of them described the moment: 'He was an officer all alone, and as he came closer, erect and full of fire, his jet-black and long hair, and his blue uniform of a general officer made him the cynosure of all.' It was General Bee. He asked who their commander was, then rode along the line. An orderly sergeant of Jackson's, Henry Kyd Douglas, later wrote: 'General Jackson was sitting on his horse very near us. General Bee, his brigade being crushed, rode up to him and with the mortification of an heroic soldier reported that the enemy was beating him back.

"Very well, General," replied Jackson.

"But how do you expect to stop them?"

"We'll give them the bayonet," was the brief answer.

Bee galloped away and General Jackson turned to Lieutenant H. H. Lee of his staff with this message:

"Tell the colonels of this brigade that the enemy are advancing; when their heads are seen above the hill, let the whole line rise, move forward with a shout and trust to the bayonet. I'm tired of this long-range work!"'

Bee rode off to see what was left of his brigade. He could only find one of his regiments, the 4th Alabama, and they were disorganized and dispirited, all their senior officers gone. Bee appealed to them to return to the fighting under his command. It is not certain what his exact words were. The first published account appeared in *The Charleston Mercury*, quoting General Bee's principal aide. According to this, Bee turned to the Alabamans, gestured with his sword towards Jackson's line and shouted: 'There is Jackson standing like a stone wall. Let us determine to die here, and we will conquer. Follow me!' Beauregard, in his account of the battle, gives the words that are usually quoted: 'Look! There stands Jackson like a stone wall. Rally behind the Virginians!' Three days after the battle, back in Richmond, one of Beauregard's staff officers, Colonel Chesnut, was reunited with his wife and told her, and she wrote it into her diary, of 'Colonel Jackson, whose regiment stood so stock still under fire that they are called a stone wall'. Whatever the precise wording and circumstance, an enduring and legendary name had been given. And Bee's call worked. The men of the 4th Alabama followed him back towards the enemy. Bee, still on horseback, was at the head of the leading company when they came under fierce fire from the Northern artillery. Bee was severely wounded, and an aide carried him to the rear. He died before the day was out.

It was about this time, half an hour into the afternoon, that the commanding generals, Johnston and Beauregard, finally arrived at the summit of Henry Hill. For the first time that day they were under heavy fire, but they calmly disregarded it and set about reorganizing their shattered units and getting them back into a defensive line around Jackson. Beauregard wrote: 'We found the commanders resolutely stemming the further flight of the routed forces, but vainly endeavouring to restore order, and our own efforts were as futile. Every segment of line we succeeded in forming was again dissolved while another was being formed: more than two thousand men were shouting each some suggestion to his neighbour, their voices mingling with the noise of the shells hurtling through the trees overhead, and all word of command drowned in the confusion and uproar. The disorder seemed irretrievable, but happily the thought came to me that if their colours were planted out to the front the men might rally on them, and I gave the order to carry the standards forward some 40 yards which was promptly executed by the regimental officers, thus drawing the common eye of the troops. They now received easily the orders to advance and form on the line of their colours, which they obeyed with a general movement; and as General Johnston and myself rode forward shortly after with the colours of the 4th Alabama by our side, the line that had fought all morning, and had fled, routed and disordered, now advanced again into position as steadily as veterans.'

Johnston's account of the same incident is less colourful but almost certainly more reliable: 'When we were near the ground where Bee was re-forming and Jackson deploying his brigade, I saw a regiment in line with ordered arms and facing to the front, but 200 or 300 yards in rear of its proper place. On inquiry I learned that it had lost all its field officers; so, riding on its left flank, easily marched it to its place. It was the 4th Alabama, an excellent regiment, and I mention this because the circumstance has been greatly exaggerated.'

Division of Command

In their subsequent accounts the two generals also gave rather different versions of a vital issue that now arose. Beauregard wrote: 'As soon as order was restored I requested General Johnston to go back to Portici (the Lewis house) and from that point – which I considered most favourable for the purpose – forward me the reinforcements as they would come from the Bull Run lines below and those that were expected to arrive from Manassas, while I should direct the field. General Johnston was disinclined to leave the battle-field for that position . . . I felt it was a necessity that one of us

should go to this duty, and that it was his place to do so, as I felt responsible for the battle. He considerately yielded to my urgency . . . '

Johnston's description of this conversation agrees that the suggestion came from Beauregard and that he accepted it, but makes it firmly clear that he retained command of the whole battlefield: 'I gave every order of importance,' he said.

The incident reveals their contrasting characters. Johnston was insisting that it was he who was in charge of the battle. Beauregard was claiming that, once he had arrived on the scene, the key action of the day was his. In effect, however, the division of duties was both sensible and successful. Johnston rode the mile or so back to the Portici, which gave him a wide view of most of the field of action, a more central position and readier access to the other brigades. Those that were being hurried towards Henry Hill had to pass close by the Portici, and Johnston was able to give them precise directions. Beauregard, meanwhile, was in his element – in the heat of the action, riding along the lines to shout words of praise and encouragement as the vision of glory inspired him. The men cheered him as he passed. A bursting shell killed his horse under him. General Bartow, rallying the men of his 8th Georgia Regiment and putting them in position on Jackson's left, fell with a bullet through his heart. 'With 6,500 men and 13 pieces of artillery', Beauregard wrote, 'I now awaited the onset of the enemy, who were pressing forward 20,000 strong, with 24 pieces of superior artillery and seven companies of regular cavalry.'

Beauregard was exaggerating the disparity in strengths and, in the interest of promoting his heroic image, made no mention of the very real advantages he enjoyed. There had been time to organize his line; his men were in the defensive role; the enemy had to attack uphill, across mostly open ground. And now he had 'Jeb' Stuart and his cavalrymen, who had ridden hard from the Shenandoah to be in time for the fight and had now been placed on the left of Jackson's line.

In fact, though it was not realized until much later, the Northern commander, McDowell, had already missed the best chance he was to get that day. He had imposed his plan upon the battle. He had succeeded in getting more infantrymen and

The Battle for Henry Hill, 1400 hours 21 July

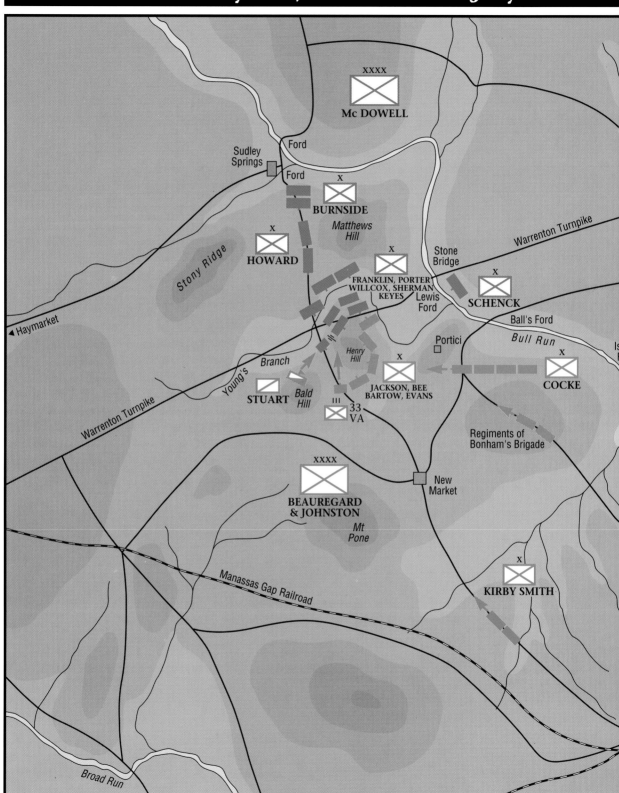

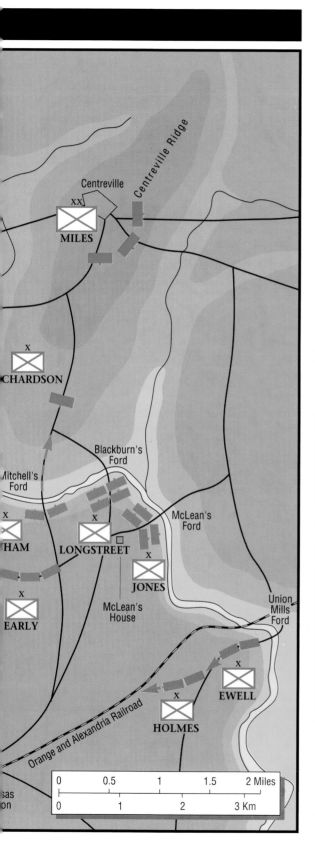

more guns to the vital place than the enemy had. Then, unaccountably, he had delayed his attack. And when he did attack, it was piecemeal. He had whole brigades available to him but he launched his men up the hill by the regiment only. One by one the regiments advanced, to be pounded by the enemy artillery as they struggled up the hill, then, as they emerged on to the plateau, to be met by a tremendous volley of fire from the infantry at short range. They would be driven back and, after a pause, giving the enemy time to reload, another regiment would be hurled forward to meet the same reception. Jackson had no need to order his threatened bayonet charge. They simply had to maintain their position, fire and re-load. He was a calming, reassuring influence, moving along the line and saying, 'Steady, men! Steady! All's well!'

Beleaguered Batteries

Early on in the Henry Hill engagement, McDowell made a serious tactical error. He ordered two of his best batteries, those of Charles Griffin and

▲ *The irrepressible 'Jeb' Stuart, who led the only effective cavalry unit involved in the battle, turned up on the left of Jackson's line; charged and dispersed the 11th* *New York Regiment; and later told Jubal Early that if he attacked now the enemy might well break, which is exactly what happened. (Anne S. K. Brown Mil. Coll., BUL)*

71

J. B. Ricketts, to advance to a position near to the Henry House, from which they could batter the Southern line at close range. These were batteries of the regular US army, efficient and ably commanded. From the very beginning of the battle they had been actively engaged, directing their fire at Evans's Brigade on Matthews Hill, then advancing on to that hill to hit the enemy positions on Henry Hill. Griffin had had one of his guns disabled, but Captain James Ricketts's battery was intact – six ten-pounder rifled guns.

When they got the order to advance, the two captains asked what infantry support they would have. They were told that the 11th New York Regiment, the Zouaves, were on their way at the double. They were dubious, but the order was firm, so they dutifully limbered their guns and set off.

The Southern battery commander John Imboden could hardly believe what he saw from the top of Henry Hill. There had been a lull in the action. 'My men lay about', Imboden wrote,

▲ *This drawing by W. Momberger gives a spirited impression of the scene on the lower slopes of Henry Hill during the long afternoon, as one by* one the Northern regiments marched up the hill in an attempt to break Jackson's line. (Anne S. K. Brown Mil. Coll., BUL)

'exhausted from want of water and food, and black with powder, smoke and dust.' Then he saw the enemy batteries advancing, *unaccompanied*: 'It was at this time that McDowell committed, as I think, the fatal blunder of the day, by ordering both Ricketts's and Griffin's batteries to cease firing and move across the turnpike to the top of Henry Hill, and take positions on the west side of the house. The short time required to effect the change enabled Beauregard to arrange his new line of battle on the highest crest of the hill . . . If one of the Federal batteries had been left North of Young's Branch, it could have so swept the hilltop where we re-formed, that it would have greatly delayed, if not wholly have prevented, us from occupying the position.'

Ricketts was first up the hill, but as he approached Henry House he came under fire from sharpshooters. 'I turned my guns upon the house', he said, 'and literally riddled it.' One of the shots smashed the bed on which the widow Henry was lying. She died a few hours later, the only woman casualty of the battle. Soon after – it was now about 2 p.m. – Griffin's battery arrived, and they turned their combined fire on Jackson's line, only 200 yards away.

But the batteries were completely unprotected. The 11th New York Regiment, in their bright red Zouave trousers, moved up the hill, at the double, to support them. The Southerners held their fire until the Zouaves were on the plateau, then let them have a thunderous volley. It was frightening rather than anything else. One Virginian witness commented wryly on his comrades' marksmanship: 'I recollect their first volley. It was apparently made with guns raised at an angle of 45 degrees, and I was fully assured that the bullets would not hit the Yankees, unless they were nearer heaven than they were generally located by our people.' After that, however, the Southerners' shooting improved, and the Zouaves found themselves pinned down in a hail of fire. The two companies on their right pulled back down the hill, escaping the rifle fire but running into 'Jeb' Stuart's cavalrymen who charged among them, slashing with sabres and firing their carbines. The plateau and slopes of Henry Hill had become an inferno of fire, smoke and confusion.

Captain Imboden, firing shrapnel at the advancing Northerners, forgot to step away from the gun's muzzle: 'Heavens! what a report. Finding myself full 20 feet away, I thought the gun had burst. But it was only the pent-up gas, that, escaping sideways as the shot cleared the muzzle, had struck my side and head with great violence. I recovered in time to see the shell explode in the

▲ *Captain Charles Griffin commanded the battery of the 5th US Artillery. They were in action early, against Evans on Matthews Hill. Later, when McDowell ordered two batteries to take position near Henry* House, Griffin made no secret of his doubts about the move but obeyed the order. The result was disaster. (Anne S. K. Brown Mil. Coll., BUL)

▲ *Captain James Ricketts, commander of the 1st US Artillery, went up Henry Hill ahead of Griffin and drove the enemy out of Henry House. When the batteries were overrun he was wounded and captured. He recovered,* was released, became a brigadier general and took part – as did many of the officers on the field at First Bull Run – in the Second Battle of Bull Run in August 1862. (Anne S. K. Brown Mil. Coll., BUL)

▲*Another of Frank Vizetelli's sketches for the Illustrated London News. It was captioned: 'Attack on the Confederate batteries at Bull Run by the 27th and 14th New York Regiments – from a sketch by our special artist'. (Illustrated London News)*

▼*The fight for the guns of the two Federal batteries at Henry House became a popular subject for American artists. This was a painting by E. Jahn.*

(Anne S. K. Brown Mil. Coll., BUL)

◀ *A private of the Louisiana Tigers, a regiment raised in New Orleans. (Illustration by Michael Youens)*

▲ *A private of the Charleston Zouave Cadets. (Illustration by Michael Youens)*

enemy's ranks. The blood gushed out of my left ear, and from that day to this it has been totally deaf.'

Imboden's battery had run out of ammunition. He ran to Jackson to ask permission to retire: 'The fight was just then hot enough to make him feel well. His eyes fairly blazed. He had a way of throwing up his left hand with the open palm toward the person he was addressing. And as he told me to go, he made this gesture. The air was full of flying missiles, and as he spoke he jerked down his hand and I saw the blood was streaming from it. I exclaimed, "General, you are wounded."

He replied, as he drew a handkerchief from his breast pocket, and began to bind it up, "Only a scratch – a mere scratch," and galloped away along his line.'

Jackson was enjoying himself, getting cooler as the fighting grew hotter. The Northerners were still attacking in waves, and there were moments when it looked as though they would break through. An officer rode up to Jackson and said, 'General, the day is going against us.' 'If you think so, sir,' Jackson replied, 'you had better not say anything about it.'

A further case of mistaken identity did much to

▲*Brigadier General William B. Franklin, commander of the 1st Brigade of Heintzelman's Division, had a distinguished army career: first in his class at West Point, promoted in the Mexican War, an accomplished surveyor and engineer. At Bull Run his men, from*

Minnesota and Massachusetts, did not reach the front until the struggle for Matthews Hill was over, but after that they were continuously under fire throughout the struggle on Henry Hill. (Anne S. K. Brown Mil. Coll., BUL)

help the Southern cause. Colonel Arthur C. Cummings's 33rd Virginia Regiment wore blue uniforms. The Colonel, afraid that his men would break and run if they were held in position any longer, ordered them to advance towards the guns of Ricketts and Griffin. Griffin saw them coming and swung two of his guns round and had them loaded with canister. Just as he was about to fire, his superior officer, Major William F. Barry, shouted, 'Captain, don't fire there; those are your battery support.' 'They are Confederates', Griffin shouted back, 'as certain as the world, they are Confederates.' But Barry insisted, and the guns were swung back to their original line of fire. The Virginians, meanwhile, marched ever closer, in line; then halted, raised their rifles and fired a volley. 'And that', Griffin told a subsequent Board

of Inquiry, 'was the last of us. We were all cut down.' Most of their horses and many of the gunners were killed. Ricketts was severely wounded. Griffin struggled to save what he could, but Cummings and his Virginians were among them quickly to capture ten field guns and much ammunition.

McDowell was not prepared to abandon such a prize. Two regiments of Franklin's brigade, men from Massachusetts who had just reached the scene after a long march, were sent charging up the slope. They re-took the guns, but only briefly, before being driven back by Jackson and his Virginians – Beauregard with them, shouting, 'Give them the bayonet! Give it to them freely!' When the enemy fell back, he rode along his line, crying, 'The day is ours.' Moments later Heintzelman, the commander of McDowell's Third Division, led the 1st Minnesota Regiment in a counter-attack, and the Virginians were driven back yet again.

The battle swayed to and fro. Another of Heintzelman's brigade commanders, Brigadier General Orlando Bolivar Willcox, led his own regiment, the 1st Michigan, up the hill to retake the guns. Then Jackson charged and drove them down again. Willcox's men were to be in the thick of the action from now on. But Willcox himself was quickly wounded and then captured. He ran towards a line of men in blue uniforms to tell them they were firing on friends, discovering too late that they were the enemy.

Fluctuating Fortunes

So it went on for nearly two hours, at the hottest time of a very hot day – a brutal, interminable slogging-match, devoid of military finesse. The premium was on courage and endurance. Even Jackson was impressed: 'It was the hardest battle I have ever been in,' he said a few days later.

Sherman's brigade was heavily involved and his official report written four days later, gives a vivid impression of what it was like: 'This regiment [the 2nd Wisconsin] ascended to the brow of the hill steadily, received the severe fire of the enemy, returned it with spirit, and advanced, delivering its fire. This regiment is uniformed in grey cloth, almost identical with that of the great bulk of the secession army; and, when the regiment fell into confusion and retreated toward the road, there was a universal cry that they were being fired on by our own men. The regiment rallied again, passed the brow of the hill a second time, and was again repulsed in disorder. By this time the New York 79th had closed up, and in like manner it was ordered to cross the brow of the hill and drive the enemy from cover. It was impossible to get a good view of this ground. . . . The fire of rifles and musketry was very severe. The 79th, headed by its colonel, Cameron, charged across the hill, and for a short time the contest was severe; they rallied several times under fire, but finally broke . . . This left the field open to the New York 69th, Colonel Corcoran, who, in his turn, led his regiment over the crest, and had in full, open view the ground so severely contested; the fire was very severe, and the roar of canon, musketry and rifles, incessant; it was manifest the enemy was here in great force, far superior to us at that point. The 69th held the ground for some time, but finally fell back in disorder.'

The commander of the New York 79th, Colonel James Cameron (his brother was President Lincoln's Secretary of War) was killed in this action. A few days later, describing the action in a letter to his wife, Sherman said, 'I do think it was impossible to stand long in that fire.' One Southern officer turned to a friend and said, 'Them Yankees are just marchin' up and bein' shot to hell.' The key factor in all this was the admirable defensive line that Jackson had chosen when he first arrived: set back from the rim of the plateau, semi-circular in shape, allowing converging fire from various directions; backed by woodland that gave the defenders good cover.

It is hard, at least with the benefit of hindsight, to see why intelligent commanders like McDowell and Sherman persisted so long with their costly, piecemeal, frontal attacks. Sherman would not have done so later on in his fighting career. McDowell had the resources, initially, to mount a frontal assault in brigade strength – one wave of men following the other too quickly to allow the enemy time to reload and reorganize. Or he could have sent Heintzelman's fresh brigades farther round the western flank to attack the enemy's side and rear. Either of these tactics, or both applied simultaneously, would almost certainly have won him the day. But none of these options was tried. The men had not been drilled in large-formation movements. Their commanders had never handled units of this size before. McDowell simply went on hoping that his next regimental attack would bring the breakthrough.

And he was, in effect, on a diminishing spiral. His new regiments, moving up to the front, could

▶ *Another artist's impression of the scene at the height of the struggle. It depicts Colonel Michael Corcoran leading a charge of the 69th Regiment against Southern batteries. (Anne S. K. Brown Mil. Coll., BUL)*

see what was happening to their predecessors. They marched past many wounded or demoralized men, scurrying to find safety. The morale impact was powerful. It is a tribute to the calibre of these young, untried, volunteer soldiers that so many of them went on fighting for so long. But all the time, the North was losing men and confidence.

About 3 p.m. the last of Heintzelman's brigades arrived – Howard with three regiments from Maine and one from Vermont. They were hurled into the attack, then hurled back by the enemy.

McDowell had no more reinforcements on the way.

For Beauregard, on the other hand, things were very different. General Johnston was feeding him with a constant stream of support – Virginian regiments from Cocke's Brigade, two of Bonham's South Carolina regiments. Some were used to strengthen Jackson's line. Others were sent to extend his western flank. And there were more on the way.

The tide of the battle was turning.

The Battle for Henry Hill, 1600 hours 21 July

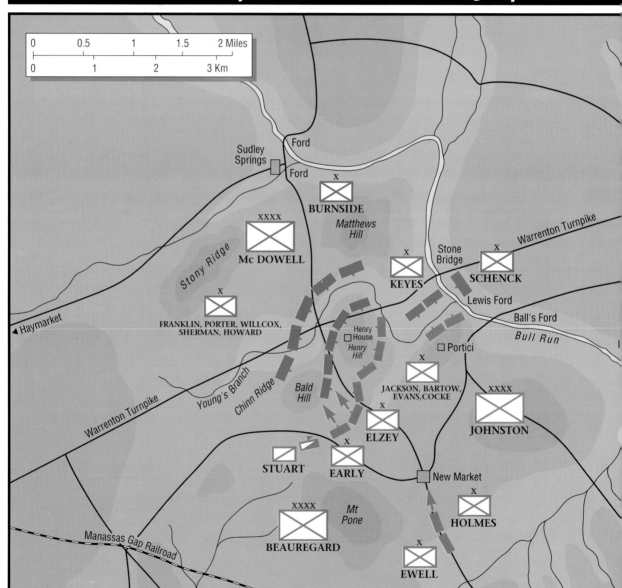

RETREAT AND ROUT

The final, clinching factor for the South was the arrival of two comparatively fresh brigades, a total of nearly five thousand men. One of these brigades was commanded by Colonel Jubal Early, the other by Brigadier General E. Kirby Smith.

Kirby Smith's Brigade, regiments from Virginia, Maryland and Tennessee, was the last part of Johnston's Shenandoah Valley army to be ferried over by train. Their journey had been much delayed, and it was not until after midday that they pulled into Manassas Junction. There they dumped their knapsacks and moved off at the double towards the battle. General Johnston ordered them to the far left of the line. It was about 4 p.m. when they arrived on the summit of Henry Hill and came under fire. Within minutes Kirby Smith had been hit in the chest by a bullet and badly wounded. His place in command was promptly taken by Colonel Arnold Elzey, a Maryland man and a graduate of

▲ *Brigadier General E. Kirby Smith commanded the 4th Brigade of Johnston's army. They were the last contingents of Johnston's to arrive at Bull Run, but they moved quickly to the left of the Southern line and got there just in time to launch a critical attack. Unfortunately, Kirby Smith could not lead the charge: he was wounded and had to hand over to Elzey. (Anne S. K. Brown Mil. Coll., BUL)*

West Point who had given distinguished service in the Mexican and Seminole wars. He led the brigade through the woods to the Chinn Ridge. Under cover of the trees they were formed into line, then advanced into the open to see the enemy directly ahead. It was what was left of Howard's Brigade after it had been driven off Henry Hill, still shaken and disorganized. Elzey ordered a volley, then a charge. Howard's men broke and ran. A few moments later a jubilant Beauregard rode up and – seeing himself for once as Wellington rather than Napoleon – cried, 'Hail, Elzey! Thou Blücher of the day.'

Jubal Early's brigade were not far behind Elzey's. Even by the standards of the day, Early was an odd man, a lonely bachelor with a short temper and a rasping tongue. His men (regiments from Virginia, South Carolina and Mississippi) called him 'Old Jube' or 'Old Jubilee'. In fact, he was no more than 44, a West Point graduate who had fought the Seminole before retiring from the army to try his hand as a lawyer and politician. He was a Virginian, another of those who argued

against secession but, when it came, threw in his lot with his state. He was to prove a very able leader in the Civil War.

So far his day had been a frustrating one with much marching to and fro, crossing and re-crossing the Bull Run without any real action. Then he was ordered towards Henry Hill. Johnston directed him to follow Kirby Smith's route and push the line even farther westwards. No sooner was he in place there than he received a message from the cavalry leader, 'Jeb' Stuart, that it looked as if the enemy were about to break and he should advance straight away. He did so, meeting minimal resistance. Beauregard now ordered the whole of his line, from the right of Henry Hill to the left of the Chinn Ridge, to move forwards. It was the beginning of the end for McDowell.

The whole of the Northern line in the Henry Hill area fell back in considerable disorder. They had been on their feet for 14 hours or so. Many had been under fire for six or seven hours. They were hot, weary and very thirsty. They had seen horrors that would haunt their memories for the

▲Colonel Arnold Elzey, from Maryland, led the charge that marked the end of all Northern hopes. They scattered the already-disorganized remnants of General Howard's Brigade. It was at this moment that Beauregard realized victory was within his grasp. (Anne S. K. Brown Mil. Coll., BUL)

▲ The eccentric but effective officer, Colonel Jubal A. Early, commanded Beauregard's 6th Brigade. Together with other commanders on the right of the line, he had spent much of the day doing little and listening, with mounting frustration, to the sounds of battle over to the west. His chance came at the last moment. It was his downhill charge from the Chinn Ridge that flung the whole Northern line into retreat. (Anne S. K. Brown Mil. Coll., BUL)

▲Frank Vizetelli's version of the panicky scene on the road to Centreville as Northern soldiers dropped their weapons and ran, getting tangled up with fleeing wagons and civilians. The flight was all the more impetuous because everyone thought the Southern cavalry were close on their heels. In fact, despite the evidence of this drawing, the cavalry never appeared. In his caption, Vizetelli wrote: 'Retreat is a weak term to use when speaking of this disgraceful rout, for which there was no excuse.' He was refused permission to accompany the next Northern army to attack into Virginia, that of General McClellan, and spent the rest of the Civil War with the Southern armies. (Illustrated London News)

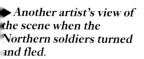 Another artist's view of the scene when the Northern soldiers turned and fled.

Final Retreat and Rout of Union Forces

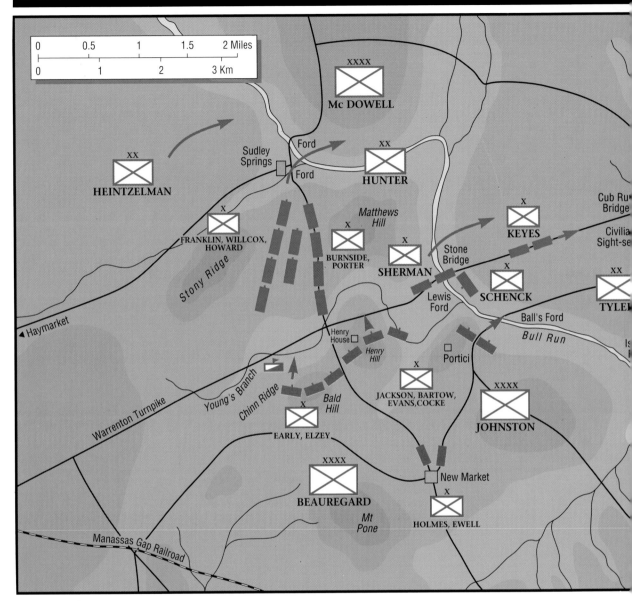

rest of their lives. Many were lost. Units were dispersed and leaderless. McDowell struggled to restore some kind of organization, but he was virtually powerless. He described the conclusion of the battle in these words: 'It was at this time that the enemy's reinforcements came to his aid from the railroad train (understood to have just arrived from the valley with the residue of Johnston's army). They threw themselves on the woods on our right, and opened a fire of musketry on our men, which caused them to break, and retire down

the hillside. This soon degenerated into disorder, for which there was no remedy. Every effort was made to rally them, even beyond the reach of the enemy's fire, but in vain . . . the plain was covered with the retreating groups, and they seemed to infect those with whom they came in contact. The retreat soon became a rout, and this soon degenerated still further into a panic.'

The picture was not all as black as McDowell painted it. A battalion of regular infantry maintained its order and covered the others' more

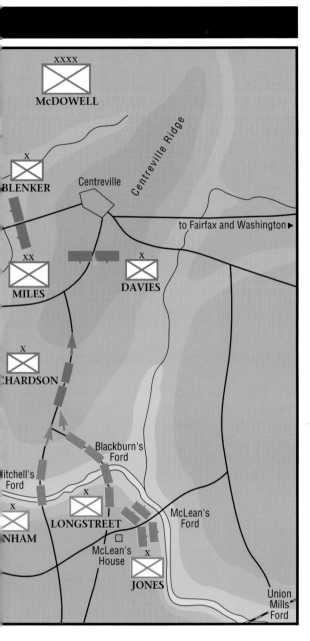

confined to my own company, and I am sure my vision was not particularly clear. General Jackson said the Second and Fourth Regiments pierced the enemy's centre. I have no doubt he knew. I have been surprised that I cannot remember any of my sensations during that turmoil, but I have a vague recollection of personal discomfort and apprehension, followed by intense anxiety for the result of the battle. Since then it has not been difficult for me to understand how much better it is for a war correspondent, in order to describe a battle vividly and graphically, not to be in it at all. I know we went in. My part of the line was driven back at first; then we went in again and fought it through, and found, when the smoke cleared and the roar of artillery died away and the rattle of musketry decreased into scattering shots, that we had won the field and were pursuing the enemy. This is not very historical but it's true.'

Most of the Northern soldiers who had been engaged in the Henry Hill fighting escaped the way they had come – by the ford at Sudley Springs or the one that Sherman had found. The real chaos, the rout, occurred a mile to the east in the area where the Warrenton Turnpike crossed a stream called Cub Run.

The Civilian Complication

The situation here was made worse by the presence of many civilian day-trippers who had driven out from Washington to spend Sunday enjoying a country picnic and a grandstand view of their army's victory. Among them were several Congressmen with their wives and families, and at first it had all been exciting and enjoyable. They were too far away to see any detail of the action, but the noise was impressive and clouds of dust and smoke assured them that they were witnessing the biggest battle that had ever been fought in North America. It was not so entertaining, however, in the late afternoon when the action suddenly and rapidly swirled towards them. They ran for their horses and carriages, fighting to get away to safety. The Southern artillery was doing all it could to encourage the confusion, and one shell hit the Cub Run bridge, overturning an army wagon and blocking the road completely. Now the

precipitate retreat. Sherman too – although he spoke bitterly about his men after the battle – made what Beauregard called 'a steady and handsome withdrawal', holding the enemy at bay.

The Southerners were also exhausted by this time, too tired and shattered to pursue the fleeing enemy with any great vigour. One of Jackson's company orderly sergeants, Henry Kyd Douglas, gave an honest and bewildered account of what it felt like to fight the battle of Henry Hill: 'I confess that I remember very little; my observation was

panic was total. Soldiers threw away their rifles and equipment and ran. Army wagons and civilian carriages were abandoned. The rumour flew that the enemy cavalry were right behind them. Senator Lyman Trumbull of Illinois wrote: 'Literally, three could have chased ten thousand . . . It was the most shameful rout you can conceive of. I suppose two thousand soldiers came rushing into Centreville in this disorganized condition.'

McDowell was in Centreville before 6 o'clock that evening. The news was telegraphed to General Winfield Scott in Washington: 'The day is lost. Save Washington and the remnants of this army . . . The routed troops will not re-form.'

As the bulk of his army continued its headlong flight, McDowell struggled to organize those brigades that remained intact, that had hardly been

◀ *This painting by Alonzo Chappel depicts Colonel Louis Blenker organizing the rearguard to cover the retreat of the rest of the army and stop the enemy reaching Centreville.*

Blenker commanded the 1st Brigade of the 5th Division, and this was his only taste of action throughout the day. (Anne S. K. Brown Mil. Coll., BUL)

▲ *William Howard Russell, the distinguished 'special correspondent' for The Times of London, went to Matthew Brady's photographic studio in Washington shortly after First Bull Run to sit for this portrait. For some reason he wore the uniform of a Deputy Lord Lieutenant of Ireland. Russell was on the scene* *too late to see much of the fighting at Bull Run, but he saw the retreat and rout and wrote a vivid account of it. As a result he was not allowed to march with the next Northern advance, and for a time he was in serious danger of being lynched by outraged Northerners. He returned to England in April 1862.*

engaged at all in the day's fighting, to form a line to defend Centreville. It proved impossible, chiefly because Colonel Dixon S. Miles, whose Fifth Division had been held in reserve, had passed much of the day swigging brandy to console himself for missing the action. Miles was 57 years old, an impressive military figure with a good combat record against the Mexicans and the Indians. But he was not suited to the inactive, supporting role. By mid-afternoon he was too drunk to issue coherent orders and, in trying to mount an attack, succeeded only in offending his fellow commanders. As soon as McDowell saw the state of the man, he relieved him of command. Darkness began to fall and the stream of shattered soldiers and terrified civilians continued to claw their way along the road back to Washington. McDowell decided there was nothing he could do but follow them.

President Lincoln had gone for his usual evening carriage ride, cheered by the reports from the battlefield. After half an hour he returned to the White House to be told that a new and terrible message had been received – the army was broken and routed. According to one of his staff, 'he listened in silence, without the slightest change of feature or expression, and walked away to army headquarters'.

The Confederate President, Jefferson Davis, had not been able to wait for the news to come to him. He took the train to Manassas where he found many soldiers who had fled from the battle and who assured him that the South had been beaten. He pushed on, however, and finally found General Johnston who told him that, on the contrary, it was the North that had been defeated and routed. He was just in time to see the final moments: 'In riding over the ground, it seemed quite possible to mark the line of a fugitive's flight. Here was a musket, there a cartridge box, there a blanket or overcoat, a haversack, etc., as if the runner had stripped himself, as he went, of all impediments to speed.' Davis rode around the battlefield, congratulating the brigades of Elzy and Early, getting food sent to men who were very hungry, trying to cheer the wounded. Later, he returned to the headquarters and questioned Johnston about the day's fighting.

Beauregard arrived about 10 p.m. Between them they composed a telegram to the War Department in Richmond: 'Night has closed on a hard-fought field. Our forces have won a glorious victory ... ' Davis signed it, to Beauregard's chagrin.

Davis asked if the enemy were being pursued. Being answered in the negative, he wondered if it were now too late. They decided to order General Bonham, whose brigade of nearly five thousand men had been least wearied by the day's work, to push towards Centreville. Then they had second thoughts, fearing it would be too risky to send them forward in the dark. So Bonham was ordered to take up the pursuit at first light. By then, however, it had been raining steadily for several hours, turning streams into rivers and the roads into quagmires. There was no pursuit.

Counting the Cost

During the next few days the battlefield was combed for equipment left behind by the fleeing Northerners. There were 27 guns, including the great 30-pounder, and a lot of ammunition; more than 500 rifles and half a million rounds of ammunition; and much else besides – wagons and horses, hospital stores and food.

On both sides the losses in men were high. The South lost almost 2,000 men altogether: 387 killed; 1,582 (possibly more than this) wounded; 13 missing, either killed or captured. The losses were particularly bad among the officers. Colonel Wade Hampton's Legion was worst hit, sustaining almost twenty per cent casualties. The brigades of Bee and Jackson were not far behind with about sixteen per cent. 'Shanks' Evans's brigade, which was in the battle from start to finish, got off more lightly: 146 casualties among 1,100 men. For the North, the figures were worse: 460 men killed; 1,124 wounded; 1,312 missing, killed or captured, mostly the latter. Sherman's Brigade was worst hit, with 107 killed, 205 wounded and 293 men missing. Andrew Porter's Brigade suffered a total of 464 casualties; that of Willcox 432. Here too there were many officers among the casualties, though the proportion was not as high as in the Southern armies.

THE 'MIGHT-HAVE-BEENS'

Every major event, certainly every battle, has its intriguing imponderables – the 'if onlys' and the 'might-have-beens' that could have transformed the whole scene. First Bull Run had more than its share of them.

If the regular army of the United States had been, say, 30,000 strong at the beginning of 1861 (twice its actual size), and if – as seems likely – the great majority of the soldiers had remained loyal to the Union, Bull Run would not have happened at all. It is unlikely that the South would have dared to take up arms.

If McDowell had had, say, 5,000 regulars under his command, he would probably have won the battle. In fact, he had only one professional unit, the 14th US Infantry, a thousand men or so under the command of Major George Sykes. They fought hard and well in the battle for Henry Hill and when, in the end, the volunteer units broke and ran, it was they who held firm and covered the retreat. A brigade of such soldiers would have made a world of difference.

In all likelihood, the North would have won the battle if General Robert Patterson had been a younger and more vigorous man and if his orders from Winfield Scott had been more forceful. Patterson failed to engage Johnston's army and hold it in the Shenandoah Valley. And, having let the enemy slip away, he failed to get his own army to the battle. It was Johnston's brigades – those of Bee and Bartow, Jackson and Kirby Smith – that clinched the issue. Indeed, it is arguable that the North would have broken through and won the day if Johnston's men had not had the railway to speed their march across. Even with the help of the railway, Kirby Smith only arrived on the battlefield in the nick of time.

McDowell's battle plan was better thought-out than Beauregard's and much more efficiently implemented. In a sense, McDowell was the victim of his own superior competence. Had he failed to get his flanking movement under way – or had Beauregard's attack gone according to Beauregard's plan – the main action would have been fought in the centre of the line, with the Northern forces in a defensive role and the Southerners having to attack across the river and then uphill. Almost certainly, the North would then have prevailed.

McDowell made three very serious mistakes. Had he taken only one day, instead of two, to reconnoitre the ground and re-provision his men, he would probably have broken through the enemy line on Henry Hill and won the battle. He might well have broken through if he had ordered the first stage of the flanking march to take place on the Saturday evening. These self-generated delays gave the enemy just enough time to get brigades into position to protect his flank. Even in the early afternoon of Sunday, when he had preponderant strength around Henry Hill, McDowell might have broken the Southern line if he had attacked in brigade strength instead of piecemeal, regiment by regiment. At this vital time the Southern cause was saved by the independent initiatives of a few brigade commanders – 'Shanks' Evans, Bee and Bartow, Wade Hampton and Jackson.

The South had most of the luck. Again and again, its brigades appeared at the right spot and at the opportune moment. The best example was the final one, when Elzey's onslaught was followed immediately by that of Jubal Early, provoking the retreat that soon became a rout. Before that, for two or three hours, the issue was delicately poised and could have gone either way.

The commanding generals on both sides knew that it all hinged, in the end, on timing. McDowell said: 'Could we have fought a day – yes, a few hours – sooner, there is everything to show that we should have continued successful.' Johnston said

McDowell's plan would have worked 'if it had been made a day or two sooner'.

Consequences

The North had been entirely confident of victory and was now utterly shocked by defeat. Some clergymen said they had been punished by God for starting the battle on the Sabbath. Most people looked for someone to blame. Patterson was the obvious scapegoat. He was roundly condemned, then allowed to disappear into retirement – his three months' service was up anyway. Miles, too, was disgraced. A court of inquiry found him guilty of drunkenness, and he never again received a command of any importance. General Tyler was luckier. His performance before and during the battle had been studiously unhelpful – aggressive at Blackburn's Ford when his orders told him to be cautious, over-cautious when the battle was on and aggression was called for. But he kept his rank and remained in the army for three more years, never distinguishing himself but doing what he could along the way to discredit McDowell.

McDowell himself was demoted within four weeks and replaced by the North's new hope, General George B. McClellan. McDowell continued to serve, though he was never again given an independent command of any significance. He took it with his usual good grace. Meeting *The Times* correspondent, William Howard Russell, who was greatly hated for his vivid account of the rout, he said: 'I must confess I am much rejoiced to find you are as much abused as I have been. I hope you mind it as little as I did. Bull's Run was an unfortunate affair for both of us, for had I won it, you would have had to describe the pursuit of the flying enemy, and then you would have been the most popular writer in America, and I would have been lauded as the greatest of generals.'

Most of the Northern commanders lived to fight another day, none of them more effectively than Sherman. Initially Sherman felt sure his military career was over. He wrote to his wife: 'Well, as I am sufficiently disgraced now, I suppose soon I can sneak into some quiet corner.' But soon afterwards he was promoted to brigadier general and on his way to greater things.

In the South all was jubilation at first. Many of the soldiers thought their victory meant the war was over – the North would not dare invade again – and simply went home. The commanders, Johnston and Beauregard, issued a proclamation the grandiose style of which suggests that Beauregard was its author: 'Soldiers! we congratulate you on an event which ensures the liberty of our country. We congratulate every man of you, whose glorious privilege it was to participate in this triumph of courage and of truth – to fight in the battle of Manassas. You have created an epoch in the history of liberty and unborn nations will rise up and call you "blessed".'

Beauregard was promoted to full general the day after the battle and made the most of the lionizing that followed. Songs and marches were composed in this honour, and atrocious verses:

'Oh, the North was evil-starred, when she met thee, Beauregard!
For you fought her very hard, with canon and petard, Beauregard!
Beau canon, Beauregard! Beau soldat, Beauregard!
Beau sabreuer! beau frappeur! Beauregard, Beauregard!'

Johnston took a less self-glorifying line. 'The credit', he said, 'is due to God and our brave southern soldiers, not to me.'

Both commanders were involved in many more Civil War battles, but neither succeeded in establishing himself as a great leader. Before long they were wrangling with each other – and with Jefferson Davis – about the conduct of the battle and the failure to pursue the enemy.

One Southern commander, Brigadier General Thomas J. Jackson – who attained fame at Bull Run, earned his nickname there and was to further enhance his reputation – refused to be swept away by the prevailing euphoria. Henry Kyd Douglas wrote: 'And yet Jackson afterwards was never enthusiastic over the results of that battle; on the contrary, he said to me that he believed a defeat of our army then had been less disastrous to us. The South was proud, jubilant, self-satisfied; it saw final success of easy attainment. The North, mortified by defeat and stung by ridicule, pulled itself together, raised armies, stirred up its people, and prepared for war in earnest.'

That is precisely what happened. The Civil War went on for nearly four more years. By April 1865 more than 600,000 men had died, more than the United States has lost in any other war; much of the land, especially in the South, had been laid waste. The distrust and hatred that were created took many decades to disperse. The First Battle of Bull Run marked the end of America's innocence.

▶ *In June 1865 a monument, built by Northern soldiers, was dedicated. Its inscription reads: 'In Memory of the Patriots who fell at Bull Run.'*

▶ *Behind Henry House stands the grave of Mrs. Judith Henry who was killed, as she lay on her sick bed, by Northern gun fire.*

THE BATTLEFIELD TODAY

The Americans conserve and cherish their historical sites, and Bull Run is a good example of this. The important places in First Bull Run – Henry Hill and Matthews Hill, Chinn Ridge and the Stone Bridge – are included in what is called the Manassas National Battlefield Park in Prince William County, Northern Virginia. It is looked after by the National Park Service of the US Department of the Interior.

On the summit of Henry Hill stands the Visitor Centre, with a handsome Grecian entrance. This is open daily except at Christmas. It offers audio-visual programmes giving an outline account of both Bull Run battles, as well as maps, prints, colour slides and a range of books about the battles and the Civil War as a whole. The staff are friendly and well-informed.

You can take, free of charge, a leaflet that gives a map of the area and details of two suggested walks. The first, no more than a mile of easy going, takes you to Henry House, past the point from which the Southern guns fired on Matthews Hill in the late morning, to the Robinson House where Hampton's Legion delayed the Northern advance; then back up the hill to the spots where Jackson organized his 'stonewall' line, where Bee and Bartow were mortally wounded, and where Griffin's battery was overrun by the Virginians.

The second tour is some six miles long, a pleasant walk along gravel paths through pine-scented woods to the river and the Stone Bridge, along the riverside passing the ford that Sherman crossed, through woods and open fields to Matthews Hill, then turning southwards to return to Henry Hill along the line where McDowell's forces advanced and then retreated. There are information boards at the key points, and some of them give you, at the press of a button, taped information about the action there.

Today the route is dotted with monuments.

Henry House is rather bigger than the building there in 1861. On one side of the house is Judith Henry's grave: on the other is a stone monument – 'In memory of the Patriots who fell at Bull Run' – built by the US Army and dedicated on 13 June 1865. Some 200 yards away, an inscribed stone marks the spot where Colonel Bartow, 'The first Confederate officer to give his life on the field', was killed. This was placed here in 1936. Two years later the State of Virginia commissioned the equestrian statue of 'Stonewall' Jackson that dominates the plateau. Close by is an inscribed memorial stone to General Bee, set here in 1939.

Across the battlefield, six-pounder canon of the period, smooth-bore and rifled, attended by their caissons, indicate the positions from which Ricketts, Griffin and Imboden and others pounded the enemy.

There is a house where the Robinson House stood, again slightly bigger than the original. The house of the freed slave survived First Bull Run surprisingly well, but was badly damaged and looted by Northern soldiers during the Second Battle of Bull Run. After the war Robinson asked for compensation, and Congress voted him $1,249. The lane up the house from the Turnpike is much as it must have been in the late morning of 21 July 1861 when Heintzelman's regiments fought their way forward, convinced that victory would soon be theirs.

▶ *Henry House today, rather bigger than it was in 1861. The guns and caissons are sited where the great struggle took place in the mid-afternoon.*

▶ *A fine equestrian statue of 'Stonewall' Jackson marks the spot where he formed the defensive line that repelled all Northern assaults.*

CHRONOLOGY

1776   The American colonies declare themselves independent of Britain.

1783   Britain recognizes the independence of the United States.

1812–14   War with Britain.

1846–8   The Mexican War.

1852   *Uncle Tom's Cabin* published.

1859   John Brown raids Harpers Ferry, is tried and hanged.

1860 November: Abraham Lincoln elected President.

December: South Carolina votes to secede from the Union.

1861 January: Six more Southern states vote to secede.

8 February: The break-away states unite to form a new country, the Confederate States of America.

9 February: Jefferson Davis elected President of the CSA.

4 March: Lincoln sworn in as President of the USA.

6 March: Davis calls for 100,000 volunteer soldiers.

12 April: Beauregard's guns open fire on the Union garrison at Fort Sumter; within two days the fort surrenders.

To First Bull Run, 1861

15 April: Lincoln calls for 75,000 volunteer soldiers.

23 May: Virginia votes to secede; North Carolina, Tennessee and Arkansas also secede at this time.

27 May: McDowell is given command of the army that is to invade Virginia.

29 June: Lincoln's Cabinet agrees to McDowell's plan of attack.

16 July: McDowell's march to Bull Run begins.

17 July: Johnston receives Beauregard's call to hurry to Manassas.

18 July: Johnston's army begins to move. Action at Blackburn's Ford.

19 July: Jackson's brigade arrives at Manassas.

19/20 July: McDowell reconnoitres a route for his flanking movement, then gives his battle orders. Johnston joins Beauregard and agrees to his battle plan.

The battle, 21 July (times often approximate only)

2 a.m.   Tyler's division begins to move off.

6 a.m.   First canon shots fired across Bull Run.

9 a.m.   Evans moves to Matthews Hill.

9.15 a.m.   Evans opens fire on Burnside's brigade.

10 a.m.   Bee and Bartow arrive to support Evans.

11 a.m.   Sherman crosses Bull Run and marches towards Matthews Hill. The Southerners pull back to Henry Hill.

11.30 a.m.   Jackson takes up his position on the top of Henry Hill.

12 noon   Johnston and Beauregard decide to move to Henry Hill.

11.30 a.m. to 4.30 p.m.   The battle for Henry Hill. Elzey charges Howard's brigade.

4.45 p.m.   Early charges Howard's brigade.

5 p.m.   Beauregard orders a general advance. The Northerners retreat, then run.

A GUIDE TO FURTHER READING

The American Civil War was the first war in history to be exhaustively described by men of all ranks. A library of books has been written about it, and the process still goes on. The war's oustanding modern, non-academic historian was Bruce Catton. The most detailed account of First Bull Run is that given by William C. Davis. The key primary source is *Battles and Leaders of the Civil War (volume 1)* edited by Robert Underwood Johnson and Clarence Clough Buel of *The Century Magazine*. First published in New York in 1887, it gives accounts of the battle by General Johnston, General Beauregard, General Fry as well as that of the artillery captain, John D. Imboden.

Other valuable sources are:

CATTON, B. — *The Penguin Book of the American Civil War*, London, 1960: a brief and balanced survey of the whole war.

— *The Coming Fury*, London, 1966: a more detailed account of the battle and the events that led up to it.

— *Reflections of the Civil War*, New York, 1981.

DAVIS, W.C. *Battle at Bull Run*, Baton Rouge, 1977: a thoroughly researched and well-written description of the whole battle, with an excellent bibliography.

— *The Fighting Men of the Civil War*, London, 1989.

EARLY, J. A. *War Memoirs*, Indiana, 1969.

HANSON, J. M. *Bull Run Remembers*, Manassas, Virginia, 1953: an entertaining and reliable account of both the Bull Run battles.

LOSSING, B. J. *Pictorial History of the Civil War (volume 1)*, Philadelphia, 1866.

SANDBURG, *Abraham Lincoln: The War Years*, New York, 1939.

SHERMAN, W. T. Memoirs of General William T. Sherman, Indiana, 1875.

▶ *After the battle a memorial was erected on the spot where Colonel Bartow received his death wound, on the summit plateau of Henry Hill. It was dedicated 'to the people of Savannah, Georgia', and inscribed with what were said to be his dying words: 'They have killed me, boys, but don't give up the fight.' (Anne S. K. Brown Mil. Coll., BUL)*

WARGAMING FIRST BULL RUN

To play the battle on a grand tactical level would require an area of 8 miles by 6 miles to be represented; from Sudley Springs in the west to Union Mills in the east, and from Centreville in the north to Manassas Junction in the south. If this sort of game is preferred, then either 2mm or 6mm figure scale would be suitable to a ground scale of 1 foot (30cm) to the mile. At such a scale the whole battle can be played out on a table not too big to be managed by most gamers.

The Confederate forces would be deployed in their historical locations covering the Bull Run fords, and the Union forces, starting from around Centreville, can be marched to battle following the historical routes; or an alternative 'what if'? scenario might be to allow the Confederates to carry out their original plan of attack either before or while the Union makes its advance. This sort of game certainly takes in the whole sweep of the countryside around Bull Run, and players may enjoy the feeling of controlling large armies, but the tactical combat may prove a little sterile and abstract for some tastes. Another disadvantage of this type of game is that players have unlimited vision across great tracts of countryside (and balloons were not used at this battle).

For those wishing to combine grand tactics with battlefield tactical combat, the best way out is to coordinate map movement with table-top combat. Unless several tables are available, minor confrontations can be decided by the weighing of tactical odds against a random factor to decide an outcome, or else the action can be frozen so that minor engagements that could possibly influence major encounters are played out first if they by chance happen at about the same time. Once a tactical encounter has been resolved, play returns to the map.

There are several board games available on Bull Run. I have used *Forward To Richmond*, which gives a reasonable simulation with regiment-sized counters. A board game can save a lot of time and effort if you choose to play from a map.

Most gamers that I know seem to prefer division-size tactical games. Indeed most commercial rules fit this framework. A ground scale of 1mm to the yard is most common as is a figure-to-men ratio of 1 to 20–33. I have personally tried more than a dozen sets of rules. The British sets tend to follow a rut of cumulative factors and short time phases in which weapons deal crippling losses far beyond their true capability, while the American sets tend to follow a board game syndrome. It is difficult to say which set is most popular of the British rules, but of the American sets it appears *Johnny Reb* has a big following. I personally prefer big battles with lots of model soldiers, alternate moves, whole figure casualties and no bookkeeping.

Tactical Games

For gamers interested in tactical refights, the actual combat area from Matthews Hill to the pine thickets at the rear of the Henry House in which Jackson placed his brigade is about 2,500 yards. The length of the combat area from the Stone Bridge to the Chinn House is about 3,500 yards. At 50 yards to the inch (2.5cm), the entire battle can be fought on a table 6 feet by 4 feet. The most suitable figure scale here is 6, 10 or 15mm. A 700–800-man regiment will occupy a frontage of 5 inches in line and will consist of 12 to 15 figures in 15mm (i.e., 1 figure represents 50 men). For 25mm figures an increase in table size is necessary to retain similarly sized regiments, and in this case 3 inches should represent 100 yards, making a table size of 6 feet by 9 feet requisite.

For those who prefer lower-level tactics at the more common ground scale of 1mm to the yard, the battle can be split easily into two main areas. The first would be the area of Evans/Bee/Bartow's combat on Matthews Hill and across Young's Branch; the other would be the climax of the battle on Henry Hill.

In refighting the battle as two set scenarios, the gamer can be assured of a more historical appreciation of the conflict since, even if the Confederates win on Matthew's Hill, the Henry Hill scenario follows historical deployment and is not affected by the result, as would be the case if Matthew's Hill was tied in with Henry Hill on the one table.

To cover the entire battle, the wargamer needs for the Confederate forces, 320 infantry, 26 cavalry and 6 model guns (assuming 1 represents 4 actual pieces); for the Union forces, 250 infantry, 5 cavalry and 6 guns. (Note that these forces represent those actually engaged and not the total strength of forces available.)

At a figure scale of 1 to 33 men for the Matthews Hill scenario, the forces scale to: Evans, 36 infantry and 1 battery; Bee, 66 infantry; Bartow, 36 infantry; Hampton's Legion, 18 infantry; plus Imboden's and Latham's batteries are required for the Confederates. And for the Union, Burnside's Brigade of 81 figures with a section of howitzers and a battery; Sykes' Regular infantry, 9 figures, and Griffin's Battery from Porter's Brigade; Franklin's Brigade, 47 figures plus Rickett's Battery and Sherman's Brigade of 96 infantry. Totals: 156 Confederate infantry figures and 233 Union infantry figures, easily within the means of most gamers.

For the Henry Hill scenario, Burnside's Brigade is removed from play, but the actual figures can be used to represent Howard's Brigade. Keyes's Brigade made a minimal effort, and perhaps one regiment might best represent his actual four. The regulars were left as a reserve on Buck Hill and could therefore be used to represent the Marines. For the start of the Henry Hill scenario the wargamer will need about 230 Confederate figures set against 400 Union figures. As the Confederate reinforcements arrive, numbers will grow to parity. For all levels of gaming, by dicing, inept commanders should be compelled to send only part of their command forward; cautious commanders advance

at half-move rates if they advance at all; and rash commanders have a better chance than others of moving their troops forward, perhaps at the double.

Morale and Training

The volunteer and militia units should have very brittle morale – high one moment, but when things begin to go wrong morale should plummet. Once broken, there should be little chance of a unit reforming, especially if losses have been over 15 per cent, and every chance that its panic will spread to neighbouring friendly units. Regulars are less likely to break but will conduct an orderly withdrawal so long as they remain in good order.

The soldiers in this battle were very difficult to manoeuver. The wargamer should restrict, by dicing, the numbers of units that may move or change formation. This is especially applicable to Union militia and volunteers. Regulars should not be handicapped in the same way.

Uniforms and Flags

A great attraction of refighting First Bull Run must surely be in the variety of uniforms that were worn. It is possible to represent each regiment wearing a different type of uniform before the dark blue sackcoats and grey/butternut jackets became standard wear in the later war years. In Sherman's Brigade the 13th New York wore grey uniforms and hats, the 69th wore blue frockcoats trimmed red but fought in white shirts, the 79th wore tartan trews and the 2nd Wisconsin wore grey frock coats and kepis. In Evans's Brigade on the Confederate side were the famous Louisiana Tigers in red shirts and blue-and-white striped baggy pants, the 4th South Carolina in grey frock coats and black hats and Terry's Texas Rangers, who were employed as scouts. For comprehensive coverage of uniforms at Bull Run I would direct readers to my article 'Sunday Picnic Uniforms', which appeared in *Military Modelling* magazine, October and December, 1987.

At Bull Run the Confederate regiments carried the 'Stars and Bars'. The St. Andrews Cross battle flag had not yet been adopted. The similarity of the

Stars and Bars with the 'Stars and Stripes' of the Federals caused some confusion, as did the wearing of both blue and grey by both sides. In addition to the National colour, Union regiments usually carried a state flag, as did some Confederates. Some units carried several flags, including regimental and presentation flags. Many companies also had guidons, so that in terms of both uniforms and flags, there is much to whet the appetite of the figure painter.

INDEX

PLACES TO VISIT

Manassas National Battlefield Park, 12521 Lee Highway, Manassas, VA 22110. Telephone: (703) 754 1861. Directions: Manassas National Battlefield Park is located 26 miles south-west of Washington DC, near the intersection of I-66 and Va.234. Hours: The Visitor Centre is open daily (closed on Christmas Day).

The Americans conserve and cherish their historical sites, and Bull Run is a good example of this. The key sites in both Bull Run battles are now preserved as part of the Manassas National Battlefield Park. Henry Hill, focus of heavy fighting in July 1861, is still cleared, though now neat and lush after decades of farming. A new farmhouse marks the sight of the old, and the peacefulness of the Chinn Ridge and Stone Bridge, now belie the violence that took place there in the opening phase of the Civil War. These and other sites on the First Bull Run battlefield can be reached by following the tours devised by the National Park Service of the US Department of the Interior.

Touring First Bull Run battlefield

On the summit of Henry Hill stands the Visitor Centre with its handsome Grecian entrance. The Centre offers audio-visual programmes giving an outline account of both Bull Run battles, as well as maps, prints, colour slides and a range of books about the battles and the Civil War as a whole. Also available at the Visitor Centre is a free leaflet that details two suggested battlefield walks.

Walk 1
The first walk is no more than one mile long and is easy going. Although this walk is self-guided, there are taped messages and interpretative signs to help tell the story of the battle as you go. The tour begins behind the visitor centre at the rebuilt Henry House. Near the house is a monument to the 'Memory of the Patriots who fell at Bull Run, July 21, 1861'. Also nearby is the grave of Mrs Judith Carter Henry, who was the only civilian to be killed during the battle. From the Henry House the trail goes north to the Confederate artillery positions overlooking Matthew's Hill – which was vital during the morning phase of the battle – and then across the fields to the Robinson House, where Wade Hampton led his South Carolina troops into the battle. The trail then loops back along the Confederate line, where General Thomas J. Jackson received his famous nickname 'Stonewall', to the site of the capture of Captain Griffen's Union canon – a turning point of the battle. The final stop overlooks Chinn Ridge where, in the late afternoon, a Confederate attack crushed the Union right and began the rout of the entire Union army.

Walk 2

The second tour is some six miles long. The route travels along gravel paths through pine-scented woods to the river and the Stone Bridge. It then moves along the riverside passing the ford that Sherman crossed, through woods and open fields to Matthew's Hill, then turning southwards to return to Henry Hill along the line where McDowell's forces advanced and then retreated. There are information boards at key points, some of which include audio messages about the action.

Today the route is dotted with monuments, many of which are also encountered on Walk 1. Two-hundred yards from the monument to the 'Memory of the Patriots', is an inscribed stone that marks the spot where Colonel Bartow, 'The first Confederate officer to give his life on the field', was killed. The stone was placed here in 1936. Two years later, the State of Virginia commissioned the equestrian statue of 'Stonewall' Jackson that dominates the plateau. Close by there is also an inscribed memorial stone to General Bee, set here in 1939.

Across the battlefield, six-pounder cannon of the period, smooth-bore and rifled, attended by their caissons, indicate the positions from which Ricketts, Griffin, Imboden and others pounded the enemy.

There is a house where the Robinson House stood but, like the Henry House, it is slightly bigger than the original. The House of the freed slave survived First Bull Run surprisingly well, but was badly damaged and looted by Northern soldiers during the Second Battle of Bull Run. After the war Robinson asked for compensation, and Congress voted him $1,249. The lane up the house from the Turnpike is much as it must have been in the late morning of 21 July 1861 when Heintzelman's regiments fought their way forward, convinced that victory would soon be theirs.

The Second Battle of Bull Run

No trip to the Manassas National Battlefield Park would be complete without a tour of the site of the Second Battle of Bull Run. In August 1862, Union and Confederate armies converged for a second time on the plains of Manassas. The naïve enthusiasm that preceded the earlier encounter was gone. The contending forces, now made up of seasoned veterans, knew well the reality of war. The battle of the Second Bull Run raged for three days, producing immense carnage (3,300 killed) and brought the Confederacy to the height of its power. Still the battle did not weaken Northern resolve. The war's final outcome was yet unknown, and it would be left to other battles to decide whether the sacrifice at Manassas was part of the high price of Southern independence, or the cost of one country again united under the national standard.

Touring the battlefield

The Second Bull Run raged over an area four times larger than the first battle. The National Battlefield Park at Manassas has devised a 12-mile tour, which covers 12 sites that featured prominently in the second battle.

1. Battery Heights

In the late afternoon of 28 August 1862, Stonewall Jackson ordered his troops to attack a Union column as it marched past on the Warrenton Turnpike in front of the hidden Confederate position north of the road. As the lead elements of General Rufus King's Union division emerged from the woods to the west, Jackson pushed his infantry forward from the distant ridge into this open field. King's troops swung to meet this attack, and for 90 minutes the two lines fought resolutely, in some places only 80 yards apart. In that short time this opening struggle of the Second Bull Run, inflicted casualties amounting to almost one-third of the 7,000 men engaged.

2. Stone House

Convinced that Jackson was isolated, Pope ordered his columns to converge upon and attack the Confederates. He was sure he could destroy Jackson before Lee and Longstreet intervened. During the fighting on 30 August, Pope made his headquarters behind this house.

3. Dogan Ridge

On 29 August, Pope's army found Jackson's men posted along an unfinished railroad grade about half a mile west of this point. Throughout the day these fields were awash with blue as thousands of Federal troops formed here for assaults against Jackson's line. Though bloody, these attacks were uncoordinated and unsuccessful. The surrounding low ridges were also the site of important Union artillery positions.

4. Sudley

Throughout the day on 29 August, Federal troops made several brutal but unsuccessful attempts to smash through the extreme left of Jackons's line, positioned on the knoll just west of here. While the fighting raged here, far to the south across the Warrenton Turnpike, Longstreet's troops arrived on the battlefield and, unknown to Pope, deployed on Jackson's right, overlapping the exposed Union left. Lee urged Longstreet to attack, but 'Old Pete' demurred. 'The time was just not right', he said.

5. Unfinished railroad

Jackson's line covered a front of about one-and-a-half miles, extending from near the Sudley Church to a point three-quarters of a mile south-west of here. The centre of his line rested in this area. The focal point of Jackson's position was the bed of the unfinished railroad. The grade is still visible running into the woods on both sides of the road.

6. Deep Cut

The morning of 30 August passed quietly. Just before noon, erroneously concluding the Confederates were retreating, Pope ordered his army forward in 'pursuit'. The pursuit, however, was short-lived. Pope found that Lee had gone nowhere. Amazingly, Pope ordered yet another attack against Jackson's line. More than 5,000 troops under the command of General Fitz-John Porter moved forward across the road into the field and crashed into Jackson's line in the area around the 'Deep Cut'. There the Southerners held firmly, and Porter's column was hurled back in a bloody repulse. A trail of about one-third of a mile begins at the road and traces the footsteps of Porter's gallant troops.

7. Groveton

The small, white frame building just west of you is the only remaining structure of the wartime village of Groveton and one of only two Civil War-era houses remaining in the park. Nearby Groveton Confederate Cemetery contains the remains of over 260 Confederate soldiers. The identity of only a handful is known.

8. New York monuments

On the afternoon of 30 August, seeing the Union lines in disarray following the repulse of Porter, Longstreet pushed his massive columns forward and staggered the Union left. A brief, futile stand on this ridge by the 5th and 10th New York Regiments ended in slaughter. In five minutes the 5th New York lost 123 men killed, the greatest loss of life in any single infantry regiment in any battle of the Civil War.

9. Hazel Plain (Chinn House)

This low stone foundation is all that remains of the Chinn House. On 30 August, Longstreet's attackers converged on this ridge, passing on either side of the house as they bore down on the Federal line. But the Federals resisted stoutly, buying time for Pope's hard-pressed forces.

10. Chinn Ridge
Stretched along this ridge, the Union troops fought desperately to delay Longstreet's advance long enough for Pope to set up a second defensive line on Henry Hill, just to the east. From here you can see a marker near the spot where Fletcher Webster, Daniel Webster's eldest son, was killed while leading the 12th Massachusetts Infantry into battle.

11. Henry Hill
Here parts of McDowell's, Porter's, Sigel's and Reno's corps made a final stand against Long-street. Taking position in the bed of Sudley Road, the Federals beat off Confederate attacks from Anderson's and Jones' divisions. Darkness brought an end to the fighting. The Union army, though beaten, was still intact.

12. Stone Bridge
Finally, under cover of darkness, the defeated Union army withdrew across Bull Run in this vicinity toward Centreville and the Washington defences beyond. Lee's bold and brilliant Second Manassas campaign opened the way for the South's first invasion of the north and possible European recognition of the Confederate government.

Nearby sites of interest:

Antietam National Battlefield Park, Telephone: (301) 432 7648. Directions: Antietam National Battlefield Park is located north of Sharpsburg on MD 65.
Antietam was one of the critical battles of the American Civil War. The fortunes of the South were riding high after the resounding victory at Second Manassas. While Bragg and Kirby Smith invaded Kentucky, Lee's invasion of Maryland was intended to maintain the Southern offensive momentum, to wrest Maryland from the Union and to win the recognition of the European powers. But his bold plan was compromised – and at the Antietam River the Army of North Virginia was fighting for its very life. Antietam not only changed the military character of the war but also the political issues as well. The Northern victory encouraged Lincoln to make public the Emancipation Proclamation in a presidential decree of 22 September 1862, to take effect from 1 January 1863. After Antietam the war went beyond mere politics: not only the maintenance of the Union but also the destruction of slavery and the survival of both Northern and Southern societies were explicitly at stake. White arrows lead the way to each stop on the National Battlefield Park's tour of this historic site. You will, however, need transport to follow the tour, which is best followed by driving between the 11 designated stops.

Chancellorsville National Battlefield Park. Telephone: (540) 323 4510. Directions: Chancellorsville National Battlefield Park is located 10 miles west of Fredericksburg VA on US 3.
Following the debacle of the battle of Fredericksburg in December 1862, Burnside was replaced as commander of the Army of the Potomac by General Joseph Hooker. Having reorganised the army and improved morale, he planned an attack that would take his army to Richmond and end the war. Although faced by an army twice his size, the Confederate

commander Robert E. Lee split his forces: Jubal Early was left to hold off Sedgwick's Fredericksburg attack, and 'Stonewall' Jackson was sent with 26,000 men in a wide envelopment around Hooker's right flank. At dusk on 2 May, Jackson's men crashed into the Federal right flank, but stiff Federal resistance slowed the Confederate advance the next day. This victory was Lee's masterpiece – but Jackson, his most capable commander, died of his wounds on 10 May. The National Battlefield Park's tour is the best way to see the key sites of this pivotal Civil War campaign. Like many other tours of this kind, you will need a car to drive between designated stops, which are often some distance apart.

Fredericksburg National Battlefield Park. Telephone: (540) 373 4510. Directions: Fredericksburg National Battlefield Park is located on US 1, Lafayette Blvd, in Fredericksburg, VA.
In December 1862, things were still confused for the Union. Antietam had been a failure for both sides, and although the battle showed that the Union army could bring the Confederates to bay, it couldn't pin them in one place long enough to destroy them. McClellan was slow in pursuing the withdrawing Lee, not acting until October 1862. Still, Lee's invasion had been stalled and repulsed. In the West, General Grant was closing on Vicksburg, and the Mississippi was under greater Union control. Lincoln appointed General Burnside to command the Army of the Potomac, and it was the latter who planned to seize and secure the town of Fredericksburg, and then take the Confederate capital of Richmond. It was an epic struggle that engulfed the Union side as it crossed the Rappahannock on December 11, encountering stiff opposition from Lee's men. The Fredericksburg battlefield tour is one that needs to be followed very carefully, as the designated route will require you to travel on some extremely busy public highways. Before embarking on your tour, call in at the visitor centre (which is located at US 1, Lafayette, Blvd) to get advice on traffic problems and suggested routes.

Gettysburg National Military Park. Telephone: (717) 334 1124. Directions: Gettysburg National Military Park is located 30 miles south of Harrisburg PA on Interstate 15.
The Confederate invasion of the Northern states was General Lee's last great gamble. By taking the war to the Union he hoped to force Lincoln into peace negotiations, or win support from the European powers who were watching events closely from across the Atlantic. Equally, Meade's Army of the Potomac needed to regain it's fighting credibility after the setbacks of Fredericksburg and saw this as an opportunity to redeem its honour. With three years behind them, North and South both boasted professional armies. The clash of 150,000 soldiers from both sides would ultimately decide the fate of a nation. Although losses were similar in number, the relative cost to the South was greater because, in this battle of attrition, they could not afford to lose the same number of men the Union could. Confederate losses were 4,637 killed, 12,391 wounded and 5,846 missing or captured, whilst the Union lost 3,149 killed, 14,503 wounded and 5,161 missing or captured. Parts of the battlefield at Gettysburg can be toured on foot, while in other sections you will need a vehicle. Call in at the visitor centre before embarking on your tour.